Zohar—Beyond the Black Whole

Compelling Evidence Superseding the Big Bang Theory

dovid krafchow

dovidHouse
publishing

Copyright © 2021 by dovid Krafchow

All rights reserved. No part of this book may be reproduced or used in any manner without written permission of the copyright owner except for the use of quotations in a book review. For more information, address: billelliot@elliot.com.

First paperback edition August 2021

ISBN: 978-1-7376-5671-5 (paperback)
ISBN: 978-1-7376-5670-8 (ebook)

www.dovidhouse.com

For
Carolica and Elise

TABLE OF CONTENTS

Preface	page 7
Introduction	page 13
Translating Zohar	page 17

Chapter One — page 25
- Why Is Zohar Important — *page 25*
- The End of Days — *page 27*
- The 777 — *page 29*
- Key to Zohar — *page 30*
- Zohar and World Peace — *page 32*

Chapter Two — page 35
- What is Zohar — *page 35*
- Aramaic Arabic Hebrew — *page 38*
- Ancient Wisdom — *page 39*

Chapter Three — page 43
- Who Wrote Zohar — *page 43*
- Where is Heaven — *page 44*
- Rebbe Shimmon — *page 47*

Chapter Four — page 51
- Daughter of Voice — *page 51*
- Where is Zohar — *page 52*
- Why Now — *page 55*
- Year Five Thousand — *page 57*

Chapter Five — page 63
- Who Am I to Reveal Zohar — *page 63*

Chapter Six — page 71
How to Read Zohar — *page 71*
Let's Read Zohar — *page 74*

Chapter Seven — page 77
Zohar from the Beginning — *page 77*

Chapter Eight — page 129
Why 2020 — *page 129*
Where to from Here — *page 134*
The Way to Peace — *page 138*
Ending War — *page 140*
Lion Lamb Pig — *page 143*
The Land of Israel — *page 146*

Chapter Nine — page 151
Ramifications — *page 151*
Science Must Adapt — *page 154*
Progress Is a Cancer — *page 157*

Chapter Ten — page 161
The Future — *page 161*
Conclusion — *page 164*
Adom Kine and the Seven Lands — *page 168*
Glossary — *page 175*

Preface

My struggle to learn the zoharic language and pristine concepts took many years; for decades the text alluded to a hidden immutable meaning beyond my understanding—I was limited to the exact translation of the words until one day Zohar opened to me and spoke. My journey in Zohar began fifty years ago, at the age of 26 when I first learned the Aleph-Bet, the Hebrew alphabet. Equipped with the 22 letters, I dove head first into the oceanic text of Torah, an overall term meaning, Teaching. Torah refers to 3500 years of endless books rectifying ideas, achieving reconciliation between differences and polishing the words into a gleam. Over the millennium, Torah has become a fine aged wine.

The Torah has also been filtered through two thousand years of Roman exile, reduced down to a fine oil able to light the way for the Jewish People, the People of the Book. Truth is bound by logic evoking questions. There is an obligation on every human being to seek the Truth and once having discovered what is true, to teach Truth to the world. How much more so the Jewish People, who are commanded to be, Lights unto the nations. In a time of darkness, only light can guide the way. The literal meaning of Zohar is Brilliance. What better remedy for our gloomy times?

There are three stages to Truth: Lips of Truth, Truth and the Truth of Truth. Zohar was saved for our time when needed most. Zohar, the Truth of Truth, represents an escape to a better reality. In our modern world, Truth is relative subjective and even dogmatic. Yet, Truth is humanity's North Star, a way to steer ourselves in a direction towards a goal while navigating life's storms. Without Truth we are stranded at sea, no direction home. The most essential Truth is, nothing comes out of nothing. Creation did not spew forth from a black hole full of nothing, but rather, we are forever connected to our source through the BlackWhole.

My intention in writing **Zohar—Beyond the BlackWhole** is to radically change the world by offering up a new perspective. I have divided my book into four sections: **First Section** explains Zohar and who I am and why I have come to reveal this information; **Second Section** is the translation to the first 13 paragraphs of Zohar, relating to the creation of our universe; **Third section** speculates on the world-wide ramifications of this information to bring about world peace; **Fourth Section** is a proof to my assertions translated directly from Zohar Chodesh.

The translations are my own, based on fifty years of committed study into the Cabala, the key to Zohar. The Cabala has been well established over the last five hundred years but until now, no one has been able to turn the key to open up Zohar. The word Zohar means, Brilliance; once the door to Zohar opens—the darkness of our world will disappear. This is not a miracle nor a ruse, this is merely the undeniable irrefutable Truth equally applied to all.

Truth is attached to the common denominator of life which is the fulcrum to a relationship with the Creator. Heaven and Earth are creation; the human being is a conglomerate of body and soul, each equally created and each unique—this is unquestionably true. Through this unique commonality, everyone is able to enter into Zohar, gleam the light that awakens the eyes and brings clarity into vision. Suddenly, world peace is possible, even inevitable. But more than write this information into a book, I have bothered myself to render many words into Hebrew and many with transliterations by which the Hebrew will become effortlessly accessible.

Hebrew, the first phonetic language, is a direct connection back four thousand years to Avraham who is the source of Hebrew, Arabic and Sanskrit through three wives and eight children. To read and recognize a Hebrew word or phrase is an open door into Heaven; the form of each letter is meaningful, full of mystery with iconic hidden knowledge gushing forth in rivulets. Also, because this information is somewhat dense, having to adjust now and again to the Hebrew will naturally slow the reader, giving more time to absorb and reflect. However, in the later part of the book, I abandon this practice hoping the reader will pick up the pace. In the end, I offer a proof from Zohar Chodesh to the fundamental concepts put forward, many of which are corroborated by science.

Zohar—Beyond the Black Whole
is evidence to a completely different reality and is the companion book to
Sex a Metaphor to History— Trump 777 and the Thousand Years of Woman
Sex is about the past while Zohar is the afterglow.

Introduction

After fifty years studying זהר/**Zohar-Brilliance**, I have become an initiate. Not that time and effort makes a master, but my understanding from זהר enables me to answer many of the inevitable questions raised by the text. This strange ancient narrative has an even stranger history, baffling the world for ages, raising further questions. Meant for the **סוף ימים/Sof Yamim-End of Days**, The זהר presents many conundrums—How did רהז come into this world? Who fathered זהר? Who first published זהר? A mythic text without an explanation or clear understanding זהר has stymied the world, until now.

Thousands of years ago, during the times of the prophets, spiritual knowledge and esoteric secrets abounded. The abundance of those claiming prophesy caused the populous to devise a test for the purported prophet. In our dark times bereft of spiritual light, replaced instead by dogmatic religion and endless charlatans vexing for money and influence, a Truth test is even more important. A hundred years ago when Einstein suggested light to be a particle rather than a wave, he challenged scientists to go out and measure the rays from the Sun bending around the orb of the moon during an eclipse, thus proving his theory. Similarly, to unlock זהר requires testing the validity of the author and his method. In 1998, I made a number of discoveries which put my life on a clear trajectory towards אמת/**Emet-Truth**. My initiation into תורה/**Torah-Teaching** began by learning the Hebrew alphabet in 1970 at age 26 (the gematria of God's Name י-ה-ו-ה/YHVH). The תורה is a four layered cake. Some nibble at the base while others indulge becoming fat with the Word; each crumb of תורה/**Torah-Teaching** leads to another crumb with a different taste and texture—one layer melds into another layer until the frosting on the top is achieved **אמת/Emet-Truth**.

Thirty years later, in 1998, I had enough information to put together a new cosmology and world history based on the קבלה/**Cabala-Receive** which I wrote into a treatise called: 26645. Advancements in technology were rampant and discoveries were coming in daily. Astronomers were revamping their conception of the universe, having recently discovered quasars beyond the limits of the known universe; scientists were scrutinizing the planets in our solar system finding new moons and unexpected anomalies—they had just discovered the second moon around Pluto, the furthest planet is our solar system. Hidden within the Kuiper Belt, Pluto remains the most mysterious of planets.

Modern day cosmologists maintain, Pluto is too small to be considered a planet. Because of her extreme distance from the Sun and her diminutive stature, Pluto did not live up the requisite of Planet and was degraded to Dwarf Planet. Four thousand years earlier, the ספר יצירה/**Sefer Yitzira-Book of Form** proclaimed: There are ten and not nine; there are ten and not eleven. This mysterious phrase refers to the planet Pluto considered too small to be counted by astronomers, thus we are reminded, there are ten from the Sun until Pluto and not nine. Also, a large planet, larger than the largest of the internal planets, lurks outside the Kuiper Belt beyond Pluto but is not considered an integral part of the solar system, thus there are ten and not eleven.

Two thousand years ago, זהר identifies this large external world as גן עדן/**Gan Aden-Garden of Eden**. Describing the human body in terms of the solar system, As above so below is a common refrain in זהר. The עיץ חים/**Etz Chiam-Tree of Life** composed of ten components is depicted in our solar system as the Sun and nine planets. These ten aspects to the עיץ חים/**Etz Chiam-Tree of Life** line up in three triangles. The smallest triangle is on top, indicating the head, with the point of the triangle facing up, corresponding to the Sun, Mercury and Venus. These three celestial bodies lack moons while the next seven celestial bodies, all have moons. Moons are a sign of life.

The next triangle has the blue Earth on the right, red Mars on the left and the point of the triangle, Jupiter is facing down. This second triangle corresponds to the two arms and the torso. The largest of the three triangles, corresponding to the legs and sex is depicted by Saturn, Uranus and Neptune with the point of the triangle facing up, thus forming the Jewish Star of six points. A combination of male and female energies comprise the three triangles but the tenth is patently woman. The nine higher aspects point but the last aspect turns, represented by the planet Pluto curving within the orbit of Neptune.

Pluto is the only planet in our solar system to enter into another planet's orbit; for twenty years out her 248 year cycle around the Sun—Pluto intertwines the circle with the line from the other nine. On February 11, 1999, Pluto crossed the threshold of Neptune's orbit returning to her own place as the ninth planet of the solar system. It was during this time, astronomers found a second moon around Pluto. Charon, possessing an elliptical orbit out into the universe like a tongue speaking words, had been discovered in 1978. The tenth aspect to the **חיםעץ/Tree of Life** described as woman, is depicted by the mouth which articulates thoughts into the words projected out into space.

There are five parts to speech portrayed by the: throat, pallet, tongue, teeth and lips. These five attributes are related to the five letters in the Hebrew alphabet written differently when occurring at the end of a word, called: **MANAZTPHACH/ ך-ף-ץ-ן-ם** the five restraints. One moon around Pluto indicated the expression of speech but two moons could only mean that three more moons must be lurking in the faraway darkness. I made this prediction in my treatise 26645 and sent it off to the Library of Congress. In 2005, seven years later, astronomers discovered the other three moons around Pluto and recently flew by in corroboration. What I had done was greater than what Einstein had done.

Einstein had predicted matter within the ray of light; I had predicted a recognizable pattern within creation disproving the very idea of the Big Bang Theory—something coming out of nothing eventually creating life. There is too much order seen in the structure of creation to have been a random event, plus within the structure there is further evidence depicting a similar structure throughout creation. Pluto rotates around the Sun every 248 years combined with the 365 days Earth rotates around the Sun equals the sum of 613, the number of commandments given to the Jewish People broken into 248 positive commandments and 365 negative commandments which is replicated by the human body into 248 limbs and the 365 connecting sinews.

זהר is the source of my information. A great light emanating from behind the BlackWhole, directing all the stars in the universe towards our world, is now available for general consumption, revealed and demonstrated through this book. Though, from ancient times the revelation of secretive texts was widely forbidden, a stance זהר confirms, yet with a caveat. When the world is falling apart, teach everything. There is no question, our world is broken, polluted, abused and used for all the wrong reasons. The time has come to rectify Mother Earth, to clarify the meaning of life and to forge ahead into the quickly approaching Thousand Years of Woman and Peace.

Translating Zohar

The Torah cannot be translated according to the literal meaning of the words but instead must adhere to the simplest meaning of the Text reduced down to logic. Literal meanings contradict, as seen in society when words are taken literally problems manifest, explanations begin and when one stands to explain he rarely sits down. The simple understanding of the Torah requires an adherence to prophesy, meaning: every word is equally important. If one word is missing or misplaced the entire prophesy is void. An improperly written word by a scribe must be buried, according to the Law. An example of faulty writings being buried can be found in the recently unearthed Dead Sea Scrolls.

Prophesy comes from Heaven where perfection is the standard and nothing is hidden but when written down in the physical world, the words are often obscured with various possible translations. Many Hebrew words have numerous meanings coupled with prophesy's predilection for alluding to mysterious forces. An example, the word מלך/**Malech** meaning **Messenger** but also means **Angel**. Prophesy comes from the heavens where angels are the Messengers of God but once transmitted to the Earth מלך/**Malech-King** has all three meanings simultaneously. Plus, the Zohar's narrative in Aramaic which uses the Hebrew alphabet, twisting Hebrew words into a completely different meaning complicating the already confusing text.

Prophesy comes from Heaven and is perfect, containing multiple meanings, each inducing a different experience, all equally valid as long as contradiction is not introduced. All opinions are valid but the most mundane understanding without harboring contradiction is considered the simple meaning of the Text. The noted commentary

רש״י/**Rashi** a thousand years ago wrote his wisdom down to be understood by a six year old brain. Literally translating the words of Torah is often obviously wrong because of the inevitable contradictory conclusion. The Commandment: If you don't keep the שבת/**Shabbat** you die would obviously decimate the Jewish People. The simple translation means to imply the penalty of Death but not the execution of Death. Each year on יום כיפור/**Yom Kippur-Day of Atonement** all penalties are washed away with prayer.

There is no authority as to what the words of the Torah actually mean. There is no contradiction in the assimilation of knowledge into one of the seventy faces of the Torah but the seventy-first opinion until infinity are wrong. Two thousand years ago when the Oral Tradition was first being committed into writing, throngs of scholars debated the different nuances to the text of the Torah and often had very public disputations but all for the sake of Truth. The tradition of disputation is famous among the Jewish People until today.

A fair question often arising as to who were these prophets that we should have faith in the fidelity of their words? The simple answer is, they required testing and if they were found to be false, they were killed. The authorities of that time did not incur death lightly; if they put to death more than one person in seventy years, the judges were considered murderers—but, for false prophesy, they would go out of their way to kill anyone who dared speak in the Name of God fraudulently. There were schools of prophets but not all prophets received prophesy.

The prophet could never be tested by a negative forecast because maybe the people repented and the spiritual decree was annulled; however, if the prophet predicts for good, the skies will rain from sunup to sundown and the rain ends an hour before the sun sets—kill the prophet because he is false, just a good weather prognosticator. Both the Torah and the Koran are completely rooted in prophesy and have protected the perfect words of the prophet without corruption. This can easily be corroborated by the exactness of these two text everywhere throughout the world to be the same.

Except for the one word דקה/**Daka** or דקא/**Daka**. Because of this imperfection in the Torah, this lost tradition of this one word, the Koran, written 2500 years after the Torah, chastises the Jewish People for having changed the Word. Seemingly indicating the Middle Eastern Sephardic traditional version is incorrect and the word דקה/**Daka** should be written with a ה/**Hey** instead of an א/**Aleph**. These two precious books of prophesy are an inheritance from אברהם/**Avraham** who came from the Tower of Babel with the ability to construct phonetic languages while the world struggled with iconic symbols. Arabic and Hebrew are considered whole languages able to received knowledge from Heaven to Earth without corruption. While the world obsesses over aliens who arise out of nothing, the Torah and the Koran describe what is true.

Therefore, in translating the תורה/**Torah-Teaching** the translation needs to take into account the incorruptibility of the text. Paraphrasing is the worst type of translation, dependent on the translator's whim and disposition. Being tethered to the Truth is the highest standard for any endeavor. Building a structure requires conforming to the basic laws of nature or else the structure will come crashing down to the ground. Spiritual structure is so much more tenuous, where the slightest misstep has huge implications in the ephemeral web of celestial beings transmitting knowledge about creation down to the Earth where the human mirror reflects our understanding back to the Creator.

The gleam of the תורה/**Torah-Teaching** has been tarnished by baseless accusations against the Jewish People for having killed god, turning these prophetic books into a mockery. Through the misrepresentation of the title from תורה/**Torah-Teaching** to Testament has poisoned each word with this Roman lie, the Father of all Lies. Veiled subsequent lies blossomed into different denominations of religion, all selling Heaven for a price. In the first American economic rescue package of 2020, the Roman Catholic Church was awarded one and a half billion dollars to the wealthiest entity on Earth, as a small business.

Only the light from זהר is able to pierce through the darkness from the long exile into ignorance, delivering the reader into the realm of peace born of clarity tethered to the Truth. With all that said, the translation of זהר is a formidable task necessitating a clear understanding of זהר. By offering up flamboyant words masking the essential nature of the idea being profited forward in the text is similar to how the Bible uses arcane and archaic language appearing to be important but without substance. The translation of זהר requires honesty plus clarity.

The key to translating זהר is knowing where the text is pointing; sometimes the text speaks from above and sometimes the text refers to below—yet in every segment of creation there is high and low, established at the very onset of creation. The **אור אין סוף/OreAin-Sof-LightWithoutEnd** is high while creation is low. Within the confines of creation according to the laws of cause and effect is established throughout the realm of high and low. The Earth is the lowest place in creation, therefore, the only place where God's original desire, to be known in low can be accomplished.

Sometimes the text of זהר looks inside the atom then suddenly changes the subject just as things are getting interesting, perhaps telling seemingly meaningless stories before turning attention to a subject completely unrelated in a hodgepodge of ideas thrown together from the Caldron of Light emanating from the far side of the BlackWhole. For all of these reasons and more, זהר is difficult to translate. The first Hebrew translation of זהר took place in 1906, the year Einstein published the paper wherein was revealed the secret to light a week before the Jewish New Year of 5666.

The text in the זהר follows the segmented yearly path forged by the Written Torah into 53 weekly portions. And like the תורה which ends with Moshe's parting from this world, so too, the text toward the end of the זהר recounts the passing of Rebbe Shimmon. The obscurity of זהר far outreaches the obvious questions produced in the Written Torah. Within the text of זהר is the supreme answer to all questions by revealing the Truth from the other side of the BlackWhole.

Sometimes parts of the זהר seem to make no sense or logical inference but only because the reader lacks the question. Knowledge of the Written Torah is essential to understanding the three levels in the Oral Tradition but particularly זהר. A hundred years ago, Rabbi Yehuda Ashlag known as the Sulaam, a great scholar in Israel was the first to translate זהר in completeness, every word translated into Hebrew. He also included within his worthy translation, a narrative rejected by other Rabbinic scholars for giving a definitive meaning to the words. The Sulaam used cabalistic terms to explain זהר which is antithetical to revealing the secret to זהר.

Recently an academic version of זהר has been rendered in English with a flowery bombastic language camouflaging the lack of knowing; thereby coming to a more literal translation colored by the translator's own biases—ultimately, a pathetic academic attempt at the Truth. Without a clear explanation concerning what the text is referring to, the Truth can never be seen, particularly concerning זהר written on seventy levels, a web of individual secrets revealed without disturbing any other threads of understanding. זהר needs to be translated from the inside out; not as an observer peering into hidden secrets—but rather looking at creation from God's Standpoint.

Another reason why זהר defies translation is because conversations tend to be fluid, taking sudden turns or even changing direction. The Light of זהר runs across the page and just as one section is grasp by the mind, the text rips away pirouetting elastic to a new dimension leaving what was just consumed, only a vapid residue of knowledge. Often the linkage between sentences does not always occur leaving the reader clinging to a cliff where the period peers precipitously into the vacuous chasm, an ionized atom seeking indifference.

As in a conversation, a web of thought and understanding merges without being able to pinpoint precisely where in the pool of thought the idea geminated. Conversations are by definition private, those overhearing the words spoken between two people are often completely misunderstood. Beyond the conversation, is the experience journeying through the pages filled with all manners of ideas and connections, like a dream come true on the pages of a book. Once the reader is awaken to the clarity contained within the words of זהר the dream becomes a reality. Translating esoteric words requires finesse but conveying an experience is another thing.

Besides the knowledge being imparted by זהר more importantly is the experience transmuted from another dimension, sucked into a whirlpool devoid of chaos, a place defying heights. The text from זהר is a mystical tool wheeled against the all consuming lie of everything but light. Nothing stands a chance against the Light Zohar. Trying to translate זהר is like trying to translate a raging river. Simply translating the words is inadequate and paraphrasing is equally inadequate since the reader is given no context for these lofty ideas hidden beneath incoherent waves.

Until the advent of the telescope, there was no context for this arcane knowledge, but now that the secrets of the heavens have been thrust open, there is no doubt as to the meaning to זהר; this supreme knowledge took two thousand years to permeate our reality just in time to save humanity from blindly following the herd over the precipice—devotees to the Lie. The antidote to the Lie is the Truth. Truth does not easily translate, the slightest inaccuracy trembles through the meaning like a discordant note amid a symphony of perfect sound.

The perfection in Heaven is necessarily broken by connecting to the Earth, the lowest place in creation where nothing is perfect and everything is either breaking or broken. The Cohen standing at the head of the congregation breaks the blessing from Heaven by holding his four fingers in a V; the congregation, like a small child being fed, needs the blessing broken into pieces to be consumed— the Truth is no different. Amazing secrets are scattered willy nilly throughout the lengthy text of זהר revealing bits of knowledge needed to fill in the puzzle of life and make sense of it all.

Translating זהר is a heavy task but it must be done for the sake of the world. "When there are no men, stand and be a man." The knowledge of זהר has come to me through fifty years of work, day and night drilling into the hard ancient rock upon which creation is founded. The Jewish People are famous for our ability to bring water out of the rock or from beneath the ground. The תורה is considered like water, flowing from a lofty elevation then coming down to the Earth, essentially the same water.

Also, the highest brick on the wall falls the furthest. Nothing is higher in Jewish texts than זהר the Light from the far side of the BlackWhole where heaviness first congeals into a twist of light engraved with the Desire of the Creator wanting to be known is low. Eventually, זהר which was meant for the future when the End of Days is evident and will lead the way to when love overcomes avarice and respect the Earth covers the globe.

CHAPTER ONE

WHY IS ZOHAR IMPORTANT

The Jewish People are widely known as the People of the Book. Indeed, the Jewish People have produced books without end, from the first book called: **תורה/Torah-Teaching** comprised of four levels separated into gender. The **תורה של כתב/Shel Kitav-Written Torah** is male and the other three levels of **תורה** are female, known as the **תורה של פאה/Shel Peh-Oral Torah**. The Written Torah is compared to the seven-branched golden candelabra. The **דין/Din-Law** derived from the **תלמד/Talmud-Study**, is the wick, first level of the Oral Torah. The oil comes from the **מדרש/Midrash-Exposition** a word implying squeezing knowledge from the Text combined with the Law to deliver a narrative. The flame of the fire is **זהר**. But, being the highest does not necessarily mean the most important. Everything has a head but sometimes the heart's emotions and the limb's reactions and the words spoken are more important. **זהר** was important to a few initiates. Since **זהר** was written for our time **סוף ימים/End of Days**, as is clearly declared in the text, there was no need to learn this book previously. Plus, **זהר** is written in an ancient language which once deciphered makes little sense to the uninitiated. From the time **זהר** was delivered to the Earth seven hundred years ago, the Rabbis, guardians over the **תורה** proclaimed prohibitions against studying **זהר** prohibitions which continue until today. The Rabbis don't want to get burned nor to burn the house down with the Brilliance from Light **זהר** but the resulting effects from hiding the knowledge **זהר** is the secret has been lost. The Book **זהר** is a large volume over 1800 pages in small print broken up into short paragraphs sectioned into the 53 weekly segments **משה/Moshe** the

Prophet who composed the first five books, sectioned the Written Torah into weekly segments. The written letter hides a fifth dimension of knowledge called gematria. Hidden beneath the letter is a value. Since each letter has an assigned number, each word has a sum showing correspondence with other concepts.

An example of gematria, the first letter of the Hebrew alphabet is א/**Aleph** with a value of one and the next letter, ב/**Bet** with the value of two. The word לב/**Heart-Lev** is the same gematria 32 as the word כבד/**Covid-Liver** which is interesting since the heart pumps the blood and liver cleans the blood. Also, there are 32 teeth corresponding to the 32 נתיבת פליאות חכמה/**Wondrous Paths of Wisdom**. When numbers need to be written, letters are used instead which sometimes incidentally makes words. In 1999 the year in Hebrew was 5759 which made the word שטן/**Satan-Opposer**. This dance between letters and numbers is present at all four levels of Torah.

There are two invisible attributes to the written letter: the נקדה/**Nekoda-Sound** (Talmud) and טרוף/**Trope-Infliction** (Midrash). The forth element of the Torah is the קתר/**Keter-Crown** set upon certain letters but not other letters, indicating זהר. Rabbi Akiva, one of the characters peopled both in the Talmud and זהר was able to learn many laws from the placment of the crowns upon the letters. משה/**Moshe** who received the תורה from Heaven was confounded by the crowns put upon seemingly indiscriminate letters. Like the crowns upon the letters, זהר is beyond comprehension except for the elites. So why was זהר written for our time, when all is dark and hidden?

The astounding progress of technology has encouraged a global hubris resulting in the destruction of our planet for the dream of going into outer space. This is an old obsession begun four thousand years ago building the Tower of Babel on the planet Mars, as described in the Book זהר/**Zohar** and זהר חדש/**Zohar Chodesh-New**. Over these four thousand years, our world has become more physical, requiring drilling into the essence of matter to power the Earth through the workings of technology. There was a time when the world was more ephemeral, easier to draw spiritual energy down to power life. The light from the past has attenuated into the present poised for the future.

We live in darkness and ignorance. No time in human history has ever been as low as our time, a time deemed by the ancients סוֹף יָמִים/**End of Days**. Into this darkness comes the Book זהר brilliance illuminating the future. If so, why has the Book זהר just happened upon the world after two thousand years, written in ancient Aramaic mixed with ancient Hebrew? Why was the Book זהר not already refined through discussion during the last two millennium like the rest of the Oral Torah? What is the point to suddenly bring forth a seemingly obtuse obscure ancient knowledge at this time in history?

THE END OF DAYS

This ominous nomenclature, סוֹף יָמִים/**End of Days** conjures up upheaval and destruction of our planet, but that is an incorrect rendition to the meaning of the term סוֹף יָמִים. Time pictured as a line infers an end; in fact, the line of history is always ending, manifested in the continual present—the question is, when will the future happen? However, time seen as a spiral has a completely different inference. A spiral is pulled into the vortex of conclusion. Think of water going down the drain or a galaxy spiraling around a Black-Whole. The DNA spirals, the Golden Mean spirals, life spirals from birth until climactic end; even sex spirals from inspiration into action ending in climax—time also spirals.

If these are the סוֹף יָמִים then when are the beginning of days? The Torah begins with the word בראשית/**Bereshith** commonly understood as **In the Beginning**. The וונה speaks on different levels at the same time. On one side the word בראשית/**Bereshith** comes to begin time with the advent of space but on the other hand, the word בראשית/**Bereshith** comes to pinpoint the precise beginning of the seven thousand years allotted for human life on planet Earth. Like the thickening rings exacting time in the trunk of the tree, each thousand year revolution around the Sun corresponds to one of the seven orbits from the seven outer planets of our solar system, beginning with planet Earth.

The delicate weave of star beams plus planetary osculations spiraling through the solar system are embedded into the spiral of our Milky Way Galaxy. Yet, universal time is regulated from the Earth, the center of creation where the human being exercises freedom of choice on the lowest level of existence, human souls in physical bodies occupying this terrestrial world. If time were endless, then life would be equally hopeless. The Big Bang Theory exemplifies this ultimate nihilism in a scenario where the spontaneous mutation of life is a futile anomaly. The spiral of time gives purpose to life. Without purpose, life is pointless.

Now, at the end of these six thousand years of human history, the world is undergoing a purification. כבד/**Covid** in Hebrew has three meanings: **Respect, Heavy and Liver**. This plague purging sickness wiping away the innocent with the guilty, is necessary to correct the Earth; the time is coming for death to be ripped from the world while the last vestige of impurity is washed away—when God wipes the tear from each cheek. Those buried in the ground will grow new bodies impervious to sickness, living a thousand years. The Roman year 2020 is **ה'תשפ/5780** years since the first human arose from the dust of the Earth, the demarcation line between the desert and the beach of the shore.

The world is shifting into conclusion mode. The arc of our time culminates in 220 years, in preparation for the Thousand Years of Woman and Peace. Rebbe Shimmon, the author of the Book זהר who two thousand years ago saw into our time of darkness and lies, now speaks to our confusion. He wrote and compiled these words for our generation of darkness and fear. Armed with lies and deceit discrediting the existence of Truth, those who seek to further the line of the lie will eventually succumb to the curve. Transitions are always difficult but the deepest darkness gives expression to the greatest light.

THE 777

One of the undeniable signs to this transitional period before the beginning of the Thousand Years of Woman and Peace is the occurrence of the number 777. A comet crossed the Bible Belt of America in the year Trump was elected, 5777. He was seventy years, seven months and seven days when inaugurated. Lastly, when the world was about to spin out of control, כבוד/**Covid-Respect**, hit the brakes on March 11, 2020 when the World Health Organization announced כבוד/**Covid-Respect** to be a pandemic, there were 7,770,000,000 people in the world. Seven is a beloved number indicating rest.

The sixth thousandth year beginning in 220 years caps the previous six thousand years with conclusion; in the same way, the six limbs of man are satisfied once united with woman who is the seventh day of the week. The שבת/**Shabbat** Bride ends the week by blessing the new week. There are four obligatory prayer sessions set out for the 24 hours of the שבת/**Shabbat**. Each prayer session is composed of seven blessings. The first three prayer sessions produce the 777 ending the previous week. The last prayer session of seven blessings begins the new week. Four times seven is כח/**Choach-Power**. The מלך המות/**Melech Hamovit-Angel of Death** is known by the number 777.

The line of time can be stretched out to infinity but the spiral of time has demarcations delineating the old cycle from the new cycle. The Roman year 2020 was a pivotal juncture merging these two disparate times—the six thousand years of man to the Thousand Years of Woman and Peace. The תלמוד/**Talmud** says, All sevens are beloved. Love has a conclusion drawing love deeper and longer until the end is excruciating blissful. This is our time, both excoriating and blissful, the pinnacle point of human development. However, the technological glare is obscuring the power of seven.

Where the other nine components, the nine points to the three triangles comprising the Tree of Life is a collusion of male and female essential energies, the tenth attribute turns and is woman. The two lower triangles on the Tree of Life are called מדות/**Medot-Measure-**

ments the music of the emotions corresponding to the human body: two arms and torso plus two legs and sex. The third and upper triangle corresponds to the intellect made from the two hemispheres of the brain plus the third eye. Emotions find expression in the mouth through speech. The year 2020 in Hebrew is **ה'תשפ/5780**. The number eighty is denoted by the Hebrew letter **פ/Pey** which translates as **Mouth**.

The seventh day of the week, called **שבת/Shabbat-Rest** is referred to as **כלה/Calah-Betrothed**. She comes from the west pressing her little pink shoe against the horizon each Friday night, causing the congregation to turn towards the west saying **בואי כלה/Boi Chala-Come Bride**. Man is compared to the shafts of light from the Sun while woman is compared to the Moon who takes from the sunlight then delivers the glow to the Earth enabling the light of the Sun to enter directly into our eyes. It is the seventh day which ends the week through the power of seven and blesses the new week through the power of seven. All sevens are beloved.

KEY TO ZOHAR

The most feminine of all the Jewish teachings is the **קבלה/Cabala** which translates as, **Receive** a feminine attribute. The **קבלה/Cabala-Receive** is the key to **זהר/Zohar-Brilliance**. The Cabala was revealed four hundred years after the channelling of **זהר** so this essential knowledge could eventually drip down into our time. The **ימי סוף/End of Days** is when the pervading darkness is challenged by the light from **זהר**. The **קבלה** is the generic name to all the hidden teachings that are not taught but need to be independently conferred. Since the genitals of male is revealed and the genitals woman is hidden, therefore the **קבלה** which is the most hidden secret is also the most feminine of all Jewish teachings.

Three thousand years ago there were schools for prophesy in the Land of Israel but not all who matriculated actually received prophesy;

similarly, those who received the hidden secrets are not necessarily the most learned or pious—Truth is Truth, no matter whose mouth is delivering the words. The slow trickle of cabalistic knowledge has been percolating through millennia of Jewish mystics able to see the light within the darkness of exile. This sublime knowledge bust forth as the קבלה a few hundred years into the beginning of this sixth and final thousand year segment before entering into the Thousand Years of Woman and Peace.

The קבלה was first manifested in the northern mountains of the Galilee, five hundred years ago in Sfat, one of the four ancient Jewish cites, corresponding to the element of air. In Sfat, modern קבלה was born from the mouth of the Ari, a Jewish mystic who beheld a vision leading him to Sfat, Israel where spiritual seekers gathered together praying to God to send them a teacher. The Ari passed away at a young age 38 having only taught for three years. His main disciple Chaim Vital wrote the seminal books considered modern day קבלה. The focus of the קבלה is the structure of creation along with minutely measured description as to how the light of creation filters down from God to Earth.

At the same time the קבלה was being revealed, the printing press was invented causing the knowledge of קבלה to suddenly spike around the world. The rabbis ruling the Jewish world delivered dictates against the study of קבלה with the exception of privileged rabbis. But, even the privileged rabbis using the קבלה to drill into זהר were unsuccessful in their pursuit, leading themselves and others astray. Nonetheless, their work was invaluable to the coming generations. Two centuries later in Eastern Europe, the Bal Shem Tov took the knowledge of the קבלה and fed it to the common folk.

I am the end to the tenth generation since the Bal Shem Tov. After five hundred years, this accumulated knowledge stemming from the Ari through the Bal Shem Tov has drenched the world in this highly technical jargon with little application to physical life or moral behavior. The קבלה is the key to זהר. The words of זהר are meant for the End of Days. Now is the time to turn the key and open the door to אמת/**Emet-Truth.**

ZOHAR AND WORLD PEACE

This obscure ancient text was written for today to avert what seems an inevitable destruction to human life on planet Earth, the end of the world. The Earth paved over with silver and plastic skewing the image of ourselves bathed in technological light has cast an uncomfortable conclusion for the future. The lie is everywhere you look: the fake news, the false face, the illegitimate system with hidden agendas—entertainment becomes truth. In תורה/**Torah-Teaching** there is no light higher than זהר/**Zohar-Brilliance**. In this time of darkness and deception, this great light is being heralded because the time of זהר has come to fruition.

The word תורה is built from the word אור/**Ore-Light**. The fourth and highest level of Torah is זהר/**Brilliance** written by Rebbe Shimmon ben Yechoi who lived two thousand years ago, prepared through the centuries as a plate of food to be fed to the world when needed. Spiritually freeing those lost in wealth and consumed by dogma, זהר is the medicine for our time; global sickness is a result of being undernourished, fed fast false food instead—the time has come to insert the key inside the lock and open up זהר for all to see.

The way is prepared, זהר has been translated into various languages and there are many commentaries concerning זהר. The end of the six thousand years of male dominance, known as the time of יסוד/**Yesod-Foundation** when the hidden is being revealed, not just physically through science and astronomy but also spiritual secrets are being divulged. The greatest secrets are hidden inside the voluminous pages of זהר written in a collusion with obscure ancient languages. Translations are endemically colored by the imperfections and biases of the translator. To get beyond the translated word, the right side of the brain must be activated.

The right side of the brain is where the soul, which is engraved from a star connects to the human body causing animation. The right side of the brain is the bastion of sight; sight is independent from the rest of the body—our ability to see in the mind is the closest the body comes to Heaven. Using sight to uncover concepts reduced down into forms reflected throughout creation brings illumination into the world. זהר exposes esoteric concepts spoken in the mama tongue of the Jewish People, ancient Hebrew and Aramaic. Vision is the great equalizer because even a blind person can make pictures in their mind.

Behind the words of זהר is a vision of creation taken from the heavens etched into the firmament where only אמת/**Emet-Truth** resides. To bring this knowledge down to the Earth for all of humanity to bath, is the final step in satisfying the Creator's Desire to be known in low. We are the lowest generation, at war with ourselves, at war with nature even at war with the Creator. The brilliance of זהר shines a light upon the face of the darkness to awaken and refresh the eyes of creation.

In a very simple way, זהר changes everything, entering us into a new era known as the Thousand Years of Woman and Peace. Once you see the way it is, you will never again be able to see the way it was. אמת/**Emet-Truth** obliterates all opposition. Only a little bit of light is needed to dispel copious amounts of darkness. There is a safeguard in the תורה to keep the lie away. All additional knowledge compiled in the תורה של פאה/**Oral Torah** must be tethered to the written text without contradiction. זהר illuminates the original text of the Written Torah without contradicting the simple meaning of the written word.

The gematria of God's Name י-ה-ו-ה/**YHVH** is 26, replicated throughout creation in the form of 26,000 thousand light years from the center of the galaxy, the 26 thousand years Earth appears to rotate around the North Star and 26,000 miles circumference around the globe plus the Earth pulses every 26 seconds. Since the age of 26, I have been committed to studying the תורה/**Torah-Teaching** and זהר in the original language of Hebrew and Aramaic. I have made predictions based on my study of זהר concerning the nature of creation, which have proven true by science. I have answered questions posed by the זהר without contradiction. Now the question is, What is זהר?

CHAPTER TWO

WHAT IS ZOHAR

There are four markings on the תורה של כתב/**Written Torah:** letter, sound, inflection, crown. They are directly related to the four divisions in תורה: the simple explanation to the written word called תורה/**Torah-Teaching**; the compiled Laws concerning the 613 Commandments given to the Jewish People called תלמוד/**Talmud-Study**; מדרש/**Midrash-Exposition** are further extrapolations conveyed by the infliction from the sound of the Law. Lastly, זהר/**Zohar-Brilliance** the secret, pictured in the crowns upon certain letters. The letters and the crowns are scribed in the handwritten scroll תורה but the sound and inflection are invisible yet added into the books to aid proper pronunciation.

זהר answers the unasked question. Without the question, the answer seems irrelevant and therefore there was little interest in זהר until recently when time has come for the secrets of זהר to be revealed. There are various aspects to זהר threaded within the fabric of the text, scattered throughout the pages, jumping out like fish jump out of water. There is little coherent structure in זהר other than being sectioned into 53 weekly segments replicating the first Five Books of the תורה called חמש/**Chumash-Five**. The text from the Book זהר meanders from the beginning and rarely returns.

זהר/**Zohar-Brilliance** skims the surface of the תורה/**Torah-Teaching** then plunges deep into the vast caverns of hidden knowledge. In this chimerical world, floating from one place to another while discussing תורה as if removing veils from before the beautiful light exclaiming, If I came into the world only to hear these words, it would be enough. The personalities populating the text of the Book זהר also frequently kiss each other: on the hand, on the head, on the mouth. And although the world is vast, they are constantly, inexplicably meeting one another on the road going from one city to another. At times, visiting in-laws.

זהר explores the workings of the heavens in long detailed descriptions including numbering the angels and entities, describing light-beams and monumental obstructions replete with primordial serpents and demons without end. The vastness of creation is only scratched upon by זהר but from that little scratch pours out knowledge in a celestial waterfall blanketing the heavens and dripping down onto the Earth in an invisible dew. Since this deep esoteric knowledge is largely incomprehensible, there was no reason to study זהר other than curiosity, until our time, a time of deep confusion amid world-wide instability.

Another reason why the rabbis discourage the study of זהר is because there is no semblance of Jewish life within the annals of זהר but rather a small cadre of חברים/**Chaverim-Friends** living life beyond the structure put in place by the Rabbis. From the vantage point of זהר etched into the firmament, they were able to see creation from a different perspective. Big questions in זהר had little relevance to the Earth and were thus shunned by the Rabbis until a hundred years ago when the first Hebrew translation of זהר was published in 1906/5666.

The original זהר is written in ancient Aramaic threaded together with ancient Hebrew text referring to obscure ideas of little relevance to life on Earth. Also, without a clear understanding of the Written Torah, since זהר comes to comment on the Written Torah from the highest level, there is little that can be garnered by the dilettante. Yet, the זהר is so revered, many spend hours a day just reading the text without understanding. Organizations have started up over the mere visual scanning of the text from זהר. Admittedly, זהר is special, but the question remains, What is זהר?

זהר is an intricate rendering as to the workings of creation where the stars and planets collude, bringing life to the Earth. Expressed beneath the hidden veneer in words and phrases scattered throughout the text of the Written Torah. זהר unites שמים/Shamiam-Heaven with ארץ/Eretz-Earth. Time and space are explored but not in an incremental way; rather like jewels hidden just beneath the surface of the sand—incoherently scattered about. The deepest secrets hidden amid the endlessness of creation are exhumed through the brilliant light spewing from זהר declaring, God the Creator to be beyond creation, completely.

זהר illuminates how a seemingly innocent text from the Written Torah is in fact, an expression from a supernal source whose ultimate design is the Tree of Life. Though exclaimed in a haphazard way, זהר gives us the information necessary to understand how the ten components composing Tree of Life are replicated throughout creation. The Preface to Book זהר begins with an image of a thirteen petal rose. The number thirteen is the gematria אחד/Echud-One which is the foundation to the Twelve Tribes of the original Arab, Jewish and Roman nations.

According to זהר everything in existence is engraved into the original seed of creation which arose in the Mind of God, inside the Head of the King. These flamboyant descriptions have little cognizance here on the Earth and yet זהר insists, this knowledge is necessary in our time to save the Earth from utter destruction. What did the masters of זהר see in the future that would necessitate the אור/Ore-Light of זהר/Zohar-Brilliance to bring peace to the world? And, what does that mean to our concept of time and freedom of choice?

The masters mentioned in זהר were not prophets. The time of prophesy had passed. Yet, they had the ability to see into time, to see our time, the End Days. The Rabbis of that time were adroit at transforming the line into a spiral allowing the initiated entrance into time. A spiral has a destination whereas the line only wants to go Forever-More. This little twist into the line of time, a twist of fate, changes everything. The symbiotic relationship between time and space is explored throughout זהר which is a map to the past and the future, so we can plot our present place plus our purpose within creation.

ARAMAIC ARABIC HEBREW

The language of זהר is ancient Aramaic, a language dating back to the Tower of Babel from where the original One Language broke, falling to the Earth, scattering fragments of sound throughout the world. Chinese and hieroglyphics replaced the original articulated language with an iconic communication while the world struggled to put together something more direct. Aramaic is the mother tongue of the Middle East; the Phoenician alphabet was a crude attempt at a phonetic language deciphering sounds into letters—this primitive alphabet was assembled in Phoenicia just north of Israel. Avraham came from the Tower of Babel built on Mars, the Phoenician alphabet was the intermediary, a vehicle by which Avraham could transfer sublime knowledge down to the Earth.

The מגדל/**Migdol-Tower** of Babel was built on Mars through the collected vibrations from around the globe. Having lived in the Tower of Babel, אברהם/**Avraham** knew the twenty-two movements of the mouth and was able to formulate phonetic languages according to the individual nature of his two sons, ישמאל/**Ishmael** and יצחק/**Yitzchok** by expanding the Phoenician concept. ישמעאל/**Ishmael** was an extroverted child while יצחק/**Yitzchok** was introverted.

Therefore, Arabic is composed in twists and swirls, a flamboyant language dancing with emotions across the page while Hebrew is made out of blocked letters more suited for the intellect. אברהם/**Avraham** perfected phonetic language in the Middle East, using the fundamental structure of the nascent Phoenician alphabet to produce the first phonic languages in the world: Arabic, Hebrew, Greek and thereby caused a quantum leap into the future. The 22 letters of the Hebrew alphabet sounds according to the name of the individual letter, thus a phonetic language.

As a result of being able to write down precise verbiage, his two children born thirteen years apart, became the Arab and Jewish Peoples. Each became a great people and powerful nation due to their language. Hebrew is enshrined in the תורה given to the Jewish People 3500 years ago; Arabic was enshrined two thousand years later when the Koran was given to the Arab People through the Prophet Mohammad—many languages derive from Hebrew and Arabic. Linguistic experts say Indo-European languages can be traced back to small group of Hurrians. Avraham came from a place called, Ur and eventually were called Aryan.

At the end of Avraham's illustrious long life, living for 175 years, he fathered six more sons with קטורה/**Katora** and sent them off to the East giving them a language without a written form. Using elements from Arabic and Hebrew, they wrote their language into what is known as Sanskrit. Through language, אברהם/**Avraham** was able to bless the entire world with these four languages conveying supernal knowledge brought down to the Earth. Aramaic was adopted into Jewish life as the common language. When the תורה was given to the Jewish People 3500 years ago, an Aramaic translation was given alongside, known as תרגם אונקלוס/**Targum Onkelos.**

Without Aramaic, there would be no way to translate the original Hebrew, holder of delicate secrets. The Aramaic is a cruder language, not as precise, creating a veneer upon the surface of the תורה by which people could comprehend what was beneath. The Book זהר is written in Aramaic because if written in Hebrew, the light of זהר would be too much for anyone to comprehend. The Aramaic is a veil before the face of the זהר/**Ore-Light** from זהר/**Zohar-Brilliance**; the Aramaic speaks in a more common voice, a more personal language—Mother Tongue to the Semitic People.

ANCIENT WISDOM

זהר rebukes explanations trying to distill the text into an idea. The randomly dispersed knowledge, erratically scattered essential thoughts and information throughout the Text without any visible continuity are comparable to the crowns randomly dispersed amid the six hundred thousand letters from which the תורה is composed.

זהר is filled with information needed to answer questions left unanswered by the Text, Law and Exposition. The תורה is continually given to each Jewish person to study and live by; the questions left unanswered indicate unique profound gaps that when answered awakens light in the world—The אור/**Ore-Light** from זהר/**Zohar-Brilliance** can enter the window of the imagination, into a world beyond Law.

זהר is a text full of answers scattered amid a curious explanation meandering through topics with little resolution, plus lengthy clarifications concerning spiritual realities with little relevance to life on Earth. Yet, all questions about life are resolved by זהר. Even so, without a properly contrived question, the secret knowledge remains secret. Another aspect of זהר is the tantalizing voice delivered in a primal language able to bring the reader into the sacred place where זהר dwells and where the work of deciphering זהר begins. According to the Law of the תורה, the commandment to study the תורה is fulfilled by exertion.

Drilling into זהר is like drilling through the ground to find water. There are two types of water in the ground. The first is called, ground water. Ground water accumulates as a result of rain or snow seeping into the soil but is easily usurped and frequently goes dry. Deeper into the Earth are found huge underwater caverns with lakes that never dehydrate, these are deemed מים חיים/**Mayim Chaim-Living Waters**. Each word of זהר is a drop of pure water within the ethereal ocean of endless light called זהר. The תורה is compared to water, coming from a very high place drawn down into the lowest place.

Most elements transform into other elements because of extreme changes in the environment but water remains essentially the same while transiting between the three stages of matter: solid liquid gas without any appreciable loss, remaining the same essential water. זהר is oceanic, a constantly moving body of fluid full of mystery and depth. To study זהר is to ride upon a sturdy ship reduced down to a cork floating beneath the gaze of massive ebony waves. זהר is not meant to be studied זהר is meant for those willing to dive in and swim.

זהר is a road upon the Earth ascending a mountain where every curve in the road slowly unravels a new unique secret hidden within creation, happening that moment. זהר is composed of endless paragraphs like waves upon the sea or the curving road up into the clouds; זהר is immutable, unexplainable—but also undeniable. זהר speaks in brevity, explaining the unexplainable by shinning a wisdom upon the world, changing perception, bringing forth clarity. The light from זהר burns clarity into the brain and trembling into the heart. The limbs of the body become annoying.

人

CHAPTER THREE

WHO WROTE ZOHAR

Prophecy comes from the mouths of angels at the bidding of the Creator. זהר also comes from Heaven but from the mouth of Rabbi Shimmon ben Yechoi known through the acronym, רשב"י/**Rashbi** but also simply referred to as, Rabbi Shimmon author of Book זהר/**Zohar-Brilliance**. Rebbe Shimmon lived two thousand years ago under Roman oppression during the destruction of the Temple in ירואשלים/**Yerushaliam-Jerusalem**. He was of the group known as the תניים/**Tannaim-Teachers** who were the culmination from five hundred years of arranging the תורה של פאה/**Oral Torah** to be written down in his generation. The later Rabbis were called אממארים/**Amoraim-Expounders**.

During the time of Rebbe Shimmon, the משנה/**Mishna** the first written iteration of the Oral Tradition was written down by יהודה הנשי/**Yehudah HaNasi** also known as רבי/**Rebbe**. Taking six hundred tractates and reducing them down to six. רבי/**Rebbe** was the beginning of the תלמד/**Talmud-Learn**; acknowledged for his wisdom, רבי/**Rebbe** set forth the דין/**Law** in writing for the first time—the first rendering of the Oral Tradition. It had become evident עשו/**Esau** Father to Rome was going to destroy the Promised Land and cast his twin brother ישראל/**Yisroel-Israel** from their home out into the global cauldron to boil in the exile. If the Oral Tradition was not written down it would be lost. Once committed to the written word, no one can add or subtract. Later books written by the אממארים/**Amoraim-Expounders**, the גמורה/**Gemora-Finishing** would only come to explain the משנה/**Mishna-Teach**. תלמוד/**Talmud-Learn** based on משנה/**Mishna-Teach** and the מדרש/**Midrash-Book** of Exposition were written down at the same time.

Rebbe Shimmon was part of this transitional generation who first wrote down the Oral Tradition. Famous for his small cadre of followers, Rebbe Shimmon was known as בוצינא דקרדינותא/**Botzina Kardinota-Harder Than Hard** because he was able to drill into words from the תורה and reveal the essence. Rebbe Shimmon and his son Rebbe Elarzer are featured in stories throughout the תלמוד/**Talmud**. Rebbe Shimmon was known to often leave this terrestrial world, coming back thirty days later to pray his daily obligation.

Rebbe Shimmon and his son, because they were being pursued by Roman soldiers, fled to Meron in the northern Israeli mountains, opposite ancient Sfat, City of Air, overlooking the inland sea resembling the shape of a harp. For seven years father and son lived in a cave. To preserve their clothes for the שבת/**Shabbat** they would bury themselves naked in the sand while they studied. When years later, Rebbe Elarzer buried his father in that same cave in Meron, a serpent appeared at the entrance of the cave allowing only Rebbe Elarzer to be buried in the same cave some years later. Until today, people gather on the anniversary of Rebbe Shimmon's passing on לג בעומר/**Lag B'Omer—33rd day counting the Omer** to celebrate.

Rebbe Shimmon left no manuscript or disciples to further his work. Not until a thousand years later did his work come to the Earth through a Jewish mystic in Spain, Moshe Shem Tov de Leon who received these words from Rebbe Shimmon then wrote them down. After his death, a rich man came upon the manuscripts and realizing the value of the work, bought them from the widow for publication. Because the transmission process from Heaven was clumsy, there remains much minutia that scholars debate, but the explicit wisdom within the text, the uncanny ability to go right to the point is זהר.

WHERE IS HEAVEN

שמים/**Shamiayim-Heaven** is made from the three higher elements: איש/**Fire**, אויר/**Air** and מים/**Water** making the heavens ephemeral.

זהר begins with a description of how the first BlackWhole was formed becoming the womb for the stars sprayed out into a space having been previously engraved out of a HardLight. Something can not come out of nothing; but rather, the nothing of space was engraved out of the HardLight—nothing out of something. The BlackWhole resulted from the initial engraving and from the friction created within the BlackWhole manifesting heaviness, progenitor of the elements for the stars and the planets.

The scientific black hole is a depiction of all creation coming out of nothing, a black hole; but, the real description should be called, a BlackWhole in one word because on the other side of the BlackWhole is Oneness—the entirety of creation in One unified whole. Comparably, the creation of the universe is like nothing to the original Oneness. Nothing comes forth from something. The slight change of adding a W to the word Hole changes everything. This coincidence of language, since English is not a holy language, is just a coincidence but an interesting one.

Creation is embedded into the Hard Light known as אור אין סוף/**OreAinSof-LightWithoutEnd** a primordial light in a state of quiescence without beginning or end, known as, שם הגודל/**Shem HaGodal-The Great Name** of God. Our creation is ten based but the original light is infinity based with truly unlimited endless possibilities. By reducing infinity down to ten, creation was able to exist without being immediately obliterated by the higher light. The endless nature of our creation is endemically restrained by the limits of ten. The Tree of Life is made from ten luminaries, the solar system is made from the Sun and nine planets.

The Earth is formed from seven continents and three oceans; the human being is made in three triangles plus the power to articulate exact thoughts through speech and writing—since our creation is based in ten. The letter **כ/Cof** with a gematria of twenty is equivalent to כתר/Keter-Crown represents both the hand and the mouth. **כ/Cof-Hand** and **פ/Peh-Mouth** are the two primary limbs of human communication. The Torah describes the human creation from dust gathered around the globe as being formed by the Hand of God, one androgynous human being connected back to back, each unable to detect the other.

The number system reverts back to one after reaching ten. The Earth is lowest place in creation being made mostly of matter mixed with a bit soul from שמים/Shamayim-Heaven. ארץ/Eretz-Earth is the lowest place in creation and all the stars are tethered to the Earth conveying the light from the אור אין סוף/OreAinSof-LightWithoutEnd down to this world. שמים begins halfway between the Earth and the Moon, according Jewish Law.

Yet, there are many divisions in שמים and from Zohar's perspective שמים begins at the furthest outreaches of our solar system. גן עדן/ **Gan Aden-Garden of Eden** floats upon the perimeter of our solar system. The stars are pitted into the firmament of Heaven; the firmament has three categories: interplanetary, interstellar and intergalactic space. The forth level is the far side of the BlackWhole. זהר proclaims, there is no knowing beyond the BlackWhole from where the stars emerged, then goes on to describe the far side of the BlackWhole. זהר is full of information about the heavens, much of which has been corroborated by science in collaboration with astronomers.

שמים is everywhere and divisions in שמים are truly endless, composed of chambers clumped together and divided into levels where the angels dwell. The soul cannot change levels in שמים without first coming down to ארץ where, if judged poorly at the end of life, the soul will go down a level. Up and down in שמים correlates the Illumination from the Creator as elevation. The angels are constantly running to and from the light, like a moth attracted to the flame yet repulsed by the heat and unable to unite. ארץ is small but she is the only physical reality in creation. When God commanded water to seek depth, all the water in the universe was drawn down to the Earth.

REBBE SHIMMON

From the descriptions within the pages of Book זהר one might think these dialogues are happening in שמים but throughout the text this view is repudiated through continual reference to Rebbe Shimmon being in this world. זהר concludes with the passing away of Rebbe Shimmon, magnifying the question, as to who wrote זהר? The main character in זהר is Rebbe Shimmon. According to Jewish tradition, the זהר was written in Heaven after Rebbe Shimmon passed away, which explains why no text of the זהר existed for a thousand years, until channeled to ארץ from שמים.

In שמים Rebbe Shimmon is referred to as, בוצינא דקרדינותא/Botzina Kardinota-Harder Than Hard similar to משה who received the 3500 תורה years ago is called by the name, רעיא מהימנא/Riyah Mehemna-Faithful Shepherd. While on ארץ/Eretz-Earth the moments in time spent actively pursuing the תורה are retained in Heaven, therefore much of what is written in Heaven results from different associations discussing aspects of תורה while on the Earth. The original זהר is written in שמים through בוצינא דקרדינותא/Botzina Kardinota-Harder Than Hard but what was transmitted to the ארץ/Earth is the oral version in the original Aramaic language of the Talmud, a combination of Mishna and Gemora,.

Rebbe Shimmon בוצינא דקרדינותא/Botzina Kardinota-Harder Than Hard takes from his monumental work in Heaven to deliver the oral version to Earth. It is rumored, Rebbe Shimmon actually wrote a book based on each of the twenty-two Hebrew letters but only the letter ז/Zyin was delivered to the Earth. Book זהר repeatedly interrupts with explanations from conversations which happened in his previous lifetime as Rebbe Shimmon. These many conversations are blended together into an intricate weave of supernal thoughts and ideas cloaked in mystery. The knowledge of זהר percolated for generations before being delivered to the Earth, as if a baby coming from her mother's womb.

זהר remained in שמים until the people of the Renaissance in Europe open the door to the thousand years of יסוד/Yesod-Foundation focused on sex portrayed through creativity. זהר remained fallow in celestial bliss until Moshe Shem Tov de Leon opened a window into Heaven where בוצינא דקרדינותא patiently awaited an opportunity to reveal his work to the world. So, in a sense, there are three authors of the Book זהר: Rebbe Shimmon from Israel, בוצינא דקרדינותא from שמים and Moshe Shem Tov de Leon from Spain. All three colluding together to bring this essential knowledge down to the Earth to be revealed at the End Days, our time.

Words from שמים are like no other words spoken on ארץ in the same way sexual pleasure is unlike any other earthly pleasure. Generally, there are a few categories of voices coming from Heaven. The highest voice is the voice of prophesy uttered by the angels meant for the ears of the prophet who must relay the words precisely to the people of the world. Some prophesy were eventually immortalized by the written word. All in all, there are 24 books plus five scrolls comprising the Written Torah divided in three segments: תורה/**Torah-Teaching** (the first five books) נבוים/**Neviem-Prophets**; כתבים/**Kotivim-Writings**.

The תורה adheres to the geometry of the Four Letter Name of God: י-ה-ו-ה which corresponds to the four elements and the four directions and four life forms: inanimate, growing, moving and speaking. The lower three levels of תורה are crowned by the fourth, זהר. The text of the **תורה של כתב/Written Torah** is immutable; the exact text of the Book זהר remains in שמים—what we have of Zohar in this world is only a glimmer of the illumination released from Heaven. Rebbe Shimmon was not a prophet and the words he spoke from שמים are not prophecy. What Rebbe Shimmon delivered to the Earth in the form of the Book Zohar, is greater than prophecy.

T

Chapter Four

DAUGHTER OF VOICE

Besides prophesy, there is what is called בת קול/**Bat Kol-Daughter of Voice** blowing in the wind. Not everyone hears the voice and there is no requirement for those who do hear the voice. This seemingly random occurrence is used by בורי/**Borai-Creator** to intervene through שמים to make a desired change in creation. Like a writer adjusting the words to a text שמים transmits needed information down to ארץ in subtle ways not to disturb the delicate balance between light and dark or sway the expression of free choice.

Channeling the writings of Rebbe Shimmon ben Yichoi down to ארץ was done in the form of a conversation with Moshe Shem Tov de Leon. This direct connection with an ancient teacher who lived upon ארץ but was concerned enough with the human predicament not to completely leave at death, who lived in the Earth's ether unable to transmit his arcane knowledge to the Earth. The righteous always suffer because of their sensitivity to the pain in the world. The most difficult death is considered like pulling thorns from the hide of sheep which inevitably ends by ripping out the flesh, that is how the righteous leave העלום/**HaOlam-The World**.

Rebbe Shimmon was not a prophet receiving exact messages through the mouths of angels, nor was he a spirit meandering through שמים but rather a high soul with direct communication with someone who was looking for שמים and found Rebbe Shimmon. Moshe Shem Tov de Leon insisted to his end, the words of זהר are the words spoken to him from Rebbe Shimmon ben Yichoi a thousand years after having lived upon Earth. The text of זהר corroborates this conclusion. No one could have composed this text other than Rebbe Shimmon בוצינא דקרדינותא/**Botzina Kardinota-Harder Than Hard**.

Rebbe Shimmon was able to burrow into each word and concept, piercing to the very essence, releasing light into the world projected through the open window of his wisdom. Though one of the Rabbis, Rebbe Shimmon was an independent soul who spent his time on ארץ seeking the secrets of creation so he could eventually write them down in שמים delivering them to the Earth a thousand years later. From his perch above the world, Rebbe Shimmon was able to see history before history happened. He could see the darkness of our time and prepared a meal for the world in the future to satisfy our longing for the past.

Rebbe Shimmon wrote זהר to funnel much needed light into the world at this time known as סוף ימים/Sof Yamim-End Days when the world will coalesce together and practice war no more. This is our time; we can accomplish this vision from the past—זהר is Light coming from the very beginning of creation inscribed with all the information to bring about redemption of the human being and the entire העלום/Ha-Olam-The World. Rebbe Shimmon knew the cure came before the sickness, so he prepared a strong medicine for our time, which is why זהר was written.

WHERE IS ZOHAR

זהר was written in שמים from what occurred on ארץ, yet from the stories and descriptions, the place of זהר is somewhat obscured. Where did זהר arise? The answer necessitates a short explanation about the nature of creation. The four elements איש/Aish-Fire, אויר/Avir-Air, מים/Miyam-Water and ארץ/Eretz-Earth are directly connected to the Four Letter Name of God י-ה-ו-ה stacked vertically form the stick figure of a human being. Originally, the four elements stacked up according to thickness: איש-אויר-מים-ארץ/Fire-Air-Water-Earth but needing to preserve aquatic life, God commanded מים/Miyam-Water to seek depth instead of covering over the surface as is the nature of primordial waters. Therefore, water freezes from the surface instead of the center unlike all other substance.

Scientists find traces of water throughout the universe as if creation is floating in a womb of celestial embryonic fluid. Astronomers have discovered a thin mist of water covering the Moon. The water that flooded the globe four thousand years ago came from the planet Mars whose waters had not been commanded to seek depth and therefore only covered the Earth in a fluid veneer enough to wipe out terrestrial life. After the flood, a river of water was left in the sky. Avraham came from the Tower of Babel built on Mars and was considered עברי/**Evri-Beyond the River**.

Since time is a spiral and not a line, what transpired at the beginning of creation happened at a faster speed than the same event happening now. Also, life was more ephemeral, able to live beyond the clouds, making terrestrial travel effortless. The seven years of famine which brought the Jewish People down to Egypt also obliterated much of the delicate structure where courses spirits resided awaiting entrance into the world. In general, the Moon is the repository for souls readying to descend down to a body to begin another lifetime. However, the eventual spiral of time has made the world less hospitable to spirit.

Rebbe Shimmon lived in a time when the space above Earth was in shambles, resembling how things were on Earth. The Rabbis had the ability to leave their bodies and ascend into the heavens bounded by the half way point between Earth and Moon. There they could easily move from one place to another, meeting each other on the road because the multitude was only found upon the terrestrial ground. This succulent firmament surrounding the Earth from just after the Flood had dried up and was crumbling down to the ground. It was the perfect place for Rebbe Shimmon and his cadre of peers to delve into the secrets of creation.

Close to the cave in Meron where Rebbe Shimmon and his son Rebbe Elazar are interned are ancient ruins with massive pillars strewn about the remaining remnants of a large buildings, depicting how the heavens look to those able to ascend into the broken celestial world made from heavenly dew lying fallow, slowly drying into rain. Perhaps those ephemeral remnants still remain but no one has the eyes to behold them and no one has the mind to comprehend this invisible ephemeral actuality closely tied to the Earth. The nature of Earth is to constantly disintegrate, so too this even refined ephemeral reality.

There are six rings in the spiral calendar begun almost six thousand years ago. Each rung in the spiral is a thousand years long. In our time, here at the apex of the spiral culminating after six thousand years related to the six outer planets are about to converged for the Thousand Years of Woman and Peace on Mother Earth. Ultimately, זהר was written in שמים, but the occurrences chronicled in זהר happened during Rebbe Shimmon's life and were memorialized in זהר because moments of תורה and אמת spoken with love, live forever.

The bigger question is where are we and who are we that זהר is needed to rescue us from this predestined time in history known as the End of Days? The fruition of the Earth happens at the end of the six thousand year male calendar when man becomes his best, so man can enter into the Thousand Years of Woman and Peace at the highest point of refinement. Living life as if time is a straight line from birth to death is simplistic and simply wrong because life is a spiral from beginning to end.

Life begins in a wide curve of time and ends in a rapid degradation of flesh as the spirit leaves the body. At the age of twenty we begin living life in decades; each decade is unique, as the body transforms from decade to decade—each decade different from the one before. The twenties are a decade of discovery, the thirties the time of strength, forties the decade of understanding, by fifty one has led enough life to be an advisor. By sixty you are either an elder or an older. Seventy is considered a full life. It takes strength to get to the eighties.

Living life as a line reduces each person into a cog in the machinery of deception trying to give purpose to a life which is devoid of purpose. Knowing where we are in the curve of our existence is important but even more essential is knowing where we are in the curve of reality, the timetable set by the Creator. After Adom eats from the fruit of the Tree of Knowledge, God asks him, איכה/Iaicha-Where Are You?

The question lingers until now, as this attenuating line of light sent from infinity goes nowhere unless, the End of Days is acknowledged.

Man is the line going nowhere; woman is a circle going round and round—only when combined does the spiral materialize. The curve of creation is feminine as is the outer planet of our solar system, the only planet to curve into another planet's orbit. We can never know where we are in the line since the line goes very fast to nowhere but once the line enters into the circle time takes on form. We are 5780 years into the spiral of time; the thousand years known as **סוד/ Sod-Secret** is when all the secrets are revealed—including the secrets contained in זהר.

זהר is revealed in our time as a final global step to be taken. זהר comes to illuminate the past present and future. The future of our planet is about to swirl into the Thousand Years of Woman and Peace. Time is not linear. In our time, much happens at a quick pace but to little avail, since time is culminating; the inner workings are moving very quickly like the inners of a clock but causing little change—yet, it is that little change that will change everything.

WHY ZOHAR

The Oral Torah was written two thousand years ago to preserve the accumulated knowledge from millennia, enabling the Jewish People to go out into the exile. During the first thousand years of Roman Exile, the Oral Tradition expanded; throughout the world, Jewish communities produced scholars from the depths of darkness revealing new insights, recording fantastic findings in endless books, some in various native languages—but, Hebrew and Aramaic are the two arms of the Torah. זהר was laying fallow in שמים waiting the appropriate time to come down and be revealed on the Earth.

The time for זהר is now, though seven centuries have passed since the writing of Book Zohar in this physical world, time was needed to get accustomed to the light for the illumination to seep into the consciousness of the Jewish People. The talmudic term used for a blind person is סגי אור/**Sogi Ore-Too Much Light**. The light has only increased during this time but the pervading darkness has kept the light distant. Over the last hundred years since זהר was first translated into Hebrew in 1906/5666 many translations have been attempted but all lacking a clear explanation as to the nature of זהר.

From his perch in the expanse between שמים and ארץ where Rebbe Shimmon and his cadre of followers travelled, the future took on clarity as the spiral of time became evident. Endemically incorporated into the spiral of time are vectors acting as measurements delineating cycles. Rebbe Shimmon could see to the end of the calendar when the darkness of lies obliterate facts and knowledge, when all that remains are glints and shards scattered senselessly about. The remnant of world knowledge remaining at the End of Days has been skewed by scholars, charlatans and fools into something other than אמת/**Truth**.

Rebbe Shimmon understood how the concept of ירידות הדורות/**Yridut HaDorat-Descension of Generations** causes אמת/**Truth** to leave the world. אמת is not visible due to the darkness. Some even contend there is no אמת. In this dark time as contrived technology spurning arrogance despoiling the world, even polluting outer space with junk in a godless rampage, only the light from זהר can save the world. But, to bring this Light to the Earth would be too much for the world to shoulder, so Rebbe Shimmon became the intermediary, he became the oral voice to זהר.

Rebbe Shimmon waited until the thousand year cycle of הוד/**Hod-Retreat** was over then at the beginning of the last thousand year time cycle called סוד/**Sod-Secret** he revealed זהר the secretive celestial writing from Rebbe Shimmon to the Earth. Just as Rebbe Shimmon was an intermediary from שמים to זהר he needed an intermediary from זהר to שמים. Rebbe Shimmon found a mystic named Moshe Shem Tov de Leon in Spain who found momentary openings in שמים to peer through and gleam a glimmer of the light. One day he found Rebbe Shimmon staring back at him.

זהר reads like a conversation. Parts of זהר reads as though being read from a book but these unattributed passages are often interrupted by past conversation from his time on Earth with his son Elarzer and his scribe Rebbe Aba along with a smattering of other personalities and names. Topics are easily replaced by new ideas generating further questions. זהר is not declarative and does not pursue answers or adjudicate law, but זהר is a flood of information derived from the author of זהר written into the firmament of שמים.

WHY YEAR FIVE THOUSAND

The question remains, if Rebbe Shimmon wanted to inform this generation on the cusp of the Thousand Years of Woman, then why deliver the information seven hundred years early? The answer is obvious, time was required to filter this heavenly information down into the Earth to be planted like a seed growing through the centuries then finally giving fruit in our time when the secrets of זהר can be revealed. This seven hundred year process has been an arduous journey from the heights of שמים down to ארץ where בורא/**Borai-Creator** wants to be known in low.

The spiritually illuminated text of זהר blinded the eyes of those who tried to peer within, becoming a yet unopened book. Later mystics tried to peer within but were unable to understand the celestial language disguised in Aramaic. Yet, there was no question as to the validity of the text and the acknowledgment that only Rebbe Shimmon could have written such a book. Moshe Shem Tov de Leon was merely a conduit, the words flowed through him getting written down on the Earth. All good writers aspire to merely be a conduit from Heaven. Humility is the fertile soil of creativity.

It would be another couple of centuries before the key to זהר would be given. Isaac Luria Ashkenazi known as the ארי/**Ari-Lion** came to teach in Sfat in Northern Israel opposite the cave where is interned Rebbe Shimmon and his son Rebbe Elarzer to teach. A small group of mystics had gathered to share their knowledge. They prayed to God to send them someone who could unravel זהר. The Ari was living in Egypt, a young man in his thirties but with eyes wide open. Everything was revealed to him. He had a vision to move to northern Israel and that is what he did. The Ari lived in Sfat for three years then passed away from the flu, a young man. He left behind a small group of Cabalists.

The ארי/**Ari-Lion** only spoke, claiming it was hard enough bringing this light to the world through speech. He wrote nothing but from his teachings in those three years in צפת/**Sfat, Israel** was born the school called קבלה/**Cabala-Receive**. The Ari is quoted as saying, I came to the Earth only to teach Chaim Vital, one of his students. Chaim Vital authored thirteen books after the ארי/**Ari-Lion** passed on. The books from Chaim Vital are the core to cabalistic thought, whose aim is to open up זהר. The קבלה in all its different manifestations from subsequent books authored by other mystics are extremely technical, tracing the dissemination of light throughout the universe.

Only the geniuses were able to open the books of the קבלה for another few centuries until the בעל שם תוב/**Bal Shem Tov** in Poland-Russia who refined the teachings of the ארי/**Ari-Lion** down to a degree where this knowledge could be fed to the people with the condition they are not allow to study זהר. The source of this prohibition comes from the תלמוד written down two thousand years ago in the tractate called ראש השנה/**Rosh HaShana-New Year** where the commandment of hearing the שופר/**Shofar-Ram's Horn** on the day of the New Year is rescinded by רבה/**Rabba**, a pillar to the generation writing down the Oral Tradition.

The Jewish New Year happens over two days in the fall commemorating the creation of the first human being. Called, ראש השנה/**Rosh HaShana-Head of the Year** these first two days correspond to the two hemispheres of the brain. Ten days later on the יום קיפור/**Yom Kipur-Day of Atonement** is considered the third eye. When the first day of ראש השנה/**Rosh HaShana-Head of the Year** falls on the שבת/**Shabbat** we refrain from blowing the שופר/**Shofar-Ram's**

Horn because רבה/**Rabba** 1500 years after the Torah was given said so. How can one man, even a great man like רבה/**Rabba** take away a Commandment from all the Jewish People and why?

The first rendering of the Oral Tradition through the Talmud was accomplished by writing in brief, encoding much of the information hidden beneath hints and cadences. The real reason behind Rabba's restriction was only known to the Rabbis of that time who understood and trusted Rabba's decision. For two thousand years, the tradition of the Jewish People is not to sound the ram's horn when ראש השנה falls on the שבת. Rabba's decree was given at the same time Rebbe Shimmon was living זהר. Rabba's decree and זהר are endemically intertwined.

The job of the Rabbis is to make confines, adjudicate boundaries and define measurements. The restriction on sounding the שופר goes far beyond the Law. The greater light was to be hidden until the right time to be revealed but not by the Rabbis. Seemingly the Rabbis should be the ones revealing the secrets. Blowing the שופר on the שבת brings about the Great Light which would be defined by the Rabbis if not restricted by רבה/**Rabba**. The Great Light is about expansion and the Rabbis are about contraction, therefore the low not the high need to define the Great Light of the future.

According to Rabba, the Shofar may not be intoned on the שבת to prevent someone who suddenly awakes on the Day of Rosh HaShana and wants to intone the Shofar but nobody else is sounding the Shofar so he can not go and ask of the Rabbis' instruction; he will have to do it his way—without instruction from the Rabbis. For God, this is being known in low and no one else should blow the Shofar as not to disturb this one individual, who because of his low status is the only one who can bring about the revelation of זהר.

God wants to be known in low, the genesis of creation. Each generation is lower than the one previous until time is about to run out on the six thousand year calendar from the first ראש השנה/**New Year** at the advent of the first human being. The Rabbis by virtue of their study of the תורה are heads of the Jewish People but God is more interested in being known by the low people, by the heel of the foot called, עיקב משיחי/**Achaiv Mechichai-Heels of Redemption**. The time has come.

A low person is the most disconnected person from society, like a homeless person. A person without family or friends, divorced from his people, from his country yet having an intrinsic connection with the Creator and the desire to forego everything to fulfill the Will of God. Walking a narrow bridge above a deep abyss, ridiculed for his path in life but admired for his tenacity and independence. The Ari taught, sometimes a very high light can come down to a very low person since the greatest light is emitted from the black pupil of the eye. Such a person am I.

CHAPTER FIVE

WHO AM I TO REVEAL ZOHAR

I was born in 1944. I remember watching my child's body being loaded into the incinerator in the crematorium at a death camp. I remember questioning God. A year later, I reincarnated into Los Angeles, California, born with the knowledge of God; born to a Jewish couple who only knew God as the word before Damn—they absolutely did not want me, yet felt forced to take me. I know this because my mother repeated this story to me well into my early teens and would always remind me how, She did not want me but she thought, I might be a girl; instead, according her description, I was not just a boy—but the ugliest baby ever born.

My mother refused to let anyone see me for the first six months of my life and as a little child when I cried, I was told, "Shut up, you don't even belong here." Worse than having parents who hate you or orphaned, is having parents live a long time and chase after you, never relenting, destroying whatever ephemeral reality a person alone in the world can erect. I went into the Navy when I was 17 and was on the ship which began the Vietnam War. A year later I got out of the service in 1965 discharge in San Francisco where LSD was still legal.

I hitch-hiked over the next five years, doing different menial jobs. Tried to understand what was going on in this strange revolutionary time. In 1970, on the heals of a tragedy, I went to Brooklyn, NY and began my ascent into Torah. Though beginning with the Aleph-Bet, I was immediately exposed to the mysterious Zohar. I had found the path to Truth in the Torah. However, there were a myriad of books I needed to master before I could approach Zohar. I quickly learned Zohar is unapproachable until the future time arrives herald by Moshiach who will teach Zohar.

Undeterred, I took on a regiment until today. For fifty years, I arise early in the morning to study for an hour or two before spending an additional hour intoning the ancient prayers. I continued this regiment throughout my very chaotic life, even being homeless, living in my car, I always managed to arise early to complete my self-imposed devotion. The difficulties in life I have experienced often brought with them miraculous redemptions, saved only by miracle. I did not depend on miracles and I did not depend on people, I lived an erratic tempestuous life. I have a profound lacking of common sense. My days turned to years becoming an ongoing dialogue with the Creator.

God is always silent in these one-way conversations. To God, Heaven and Earth are equally created moment by moment, but there is more light in Heaven than on Earth. God's response to prayer is attenuated through the intercession of the heavens dripping with dew down to the Earth where suddenly miracles occur. God is always hidden but God's effluence is forever present. Sometimes lost in the darkness of life, a greater light is revealed. My eyes became open to the words of Torah but after a lifetime of struggle I returned to California to die.

Besides the cruelty of my mother, my father was no better. He was a brutal man angry at God who beat me from a tender young age. Even before entering into grammar school, my father, armed with a leather belt dramatically ripped from his pants before beating me until I thought he would kill me. Though I survived, it was not without wounds. I did not have a Bar Mitzvah at thirteen, instead I received a kick from my father's pointed winged-tipped leather shoe causing my spine to cease up. Slowly, my spine began turning in my back. By the time I was sixty, I was almost cut in half. I knew I was dying. The doctors at the veteran hospital said I was psychotic.

I experienced the beginning of war on the flagship of the Seventh Fleet Amphibious Force set to prevent war by invading on the demarcation line separating Communist North Vietnam from Christian South Vietnam. America had established a Christian regime in the south against the godless communist in the north while the Buddhists burned themselves in the streets. Twenty-four hours before the invasion, the Pentagon bounced a message off the Moon directing us not to invade, instead to send the troops to Saigon to fight a conventional war. No one had ever won a conventional war against Vietnam, not the Chinese, not the Russians nor the French. Neither would the Americans.

Upon my release from the navy a year later, I felt embarrassed and exploited, used as an excuse to fight a proxy war against the Russians who supplied the North. My back had bent into a permanent slouch and my hair began to grey. It was 1965 and I was 21. I was in San Francisco where LSD was still legal. From 1965 to 1970 I hitchhiked 30,000 miles before finally coming to a conclusion, I would devote my life to the study of Torah because I wanted to know the Truth. People laugh at the concept of Truth since we live in world of lies where Truth has no value.

However, from the turmoil of my life and the turbulent times I lived through, I felt compelled to seek the Truth so I could know what was the correct action to take to fix the world. I learned to read and began my journey through the Hebrew books. At one point I had a library of 600 hardbound Hebrew books. Now, I only learn the Chumush, the first five books of the Written Torah and Zohar. I try to finish the Torah in the span of a year and Zohar every two years as my life spirals closer to the Truth.

There are three levels to Truth: the lips of Truth, the Truth and the Truth of Truth; or in other words: The Written Torah, the Oral Torah and Zohar. It has taken me fifty years to see the Truth illuminated in Zohar at a time when Truth is no longer expected. Perhaps, that is why Zohar was left until our time when, between scientific theory and religious dogma, the individual has no refuge but to seek the Truth. My journey into Zohar has been filled with suffering and scorn, poverty, homelessness but most of all, hope.

Constantly moving as society pushed me from one place to another, I tried to be tied above as not to fall below. But, eventually I fell into unreconcilable madness plus the rabbis had cursed me as my body was breaking in half. I was standing on the edge of insanity on one side and the end of life on the other. This is not the place to recall all the miracles and travails my life entails but at sixty my spine unwound and I moved to San Francisco where I had been raised. It is hard for me to stay in one place.

One summer day at seventy years old while living in Oregon, I experienced a sharp sudden pain on the top of my toe. I was going barefoot and looked down to see a flower-like opening as if to let out the sprite which had been hurled against me by the rabbis. Since a curse is for a lifetime, the thing could only last until seventy years, I surmised. I was suddenly let free. The opening closed at once and left no scar or hint behind. Though my spine had straightened, fifty years of contorting had left my nerves in disarray still twisting inside of me. A stricture tightening across my abdomen until once again I was painfully being cut into two, as if my body was a towel being twisted and squeezed until the last drop, now began to unwind.

What makes my life particularly unusual, is I have lived with little money and no credit which has determined my way through the world. I was not able to buy my reality, instead I took a more natural path like a drop of water yearning the sea. Life is treacherous and people can be dangerous and if you have gone mad and are unable to discern who to trust and when to do what, life becomes a torrential wave buoyed by a drunken sea. I always liked storms and have gone through typhoons and raging waves on a violent ocean. My life on land has been no different.

The life of a seeker, particularly a Jewish scholar estranged from his relatives, excommunicated from his people, a veteran of a war he never wanted to start, a vagabond often having to live in a vehicle or with other crazy people existing on the fringe, getting by on the excess of others is a story. There are many poor and lonely souls out there but my experience has been, the poorer the persons, the more truthful the person. Poverty and loneliness has a way of gnawing at the essence, witnessing something other than the polished mirrored image of ourselves. Similarly, Zohar gnaws away at our veneer and our manufactured understanding of life.

At the age of seventy three, living in my '89 Volvo Station Wagon, I returned to Los Angeles where I had been born but left when I was three. I had spent seventy years, a lifetime away. Since then, I am 76 years old now, I have found stability and a quiet life. I look back with dread. I thank God daily for the many miracles done on my behalf to get me to this place in time. There is no question in my mind, I am the low man who Rabba foresaw two thousand years ago, so Zohar would not be revealed through the rabbis and their dogmatic authority.

The rabbis of our time, recipients of 3500 years of argumentation and separation are not the ones meant to bring Zohar to the world for the purpose of שלום/**Shalom-Peace** a word which also means, Whole. Besides, as the Talmud warns, Most religious people are thieves. Rabbis already sell Zohar as a charm. Religious people of all stripes and kinds make a reality from the insubstantial plucked out the air then substantiated by believers who hold the structure together with money upon which they all depend. Rich people can buy their reality, only the poor are forced to live their God-given actuality.

The poor inevitably respond when receiving money with, God bless you. God is often on the lips of the poor and the indigent artist or craftsperson pushed out of the way by innovation towards a bottom line philosophy. True poverty is only found in those lacking knowing; knowing happens as a result of experience—the poor know more about life than do the rich. Rich people and religious people harbor a skewed sense of life; only the poor see the inevitable deteriorating nature of reality—the day and night struggle to remain alive and free. The poor are free to live what is real. The Talmud reminds us, To go high, first you must go low. Experiencing reality opens the eyes to the knowledge hidden within Zohar.

I have written many books concerning the importance of numbers and would confer on myself the number zero. The distance between zero to one is greater than the distance between one to infinity. Being autistic, I have an alienated kind of relationship with the world yet I have great love for the world and I want to give the everything I know. I have suffered to bring Zohar to the world but it was all worth the experience. Now this elder wisdom illuminating the way for the world to progress forward, together we can unite through the lowest vessel conveying the highest light.

So, who am I to reveal the Holy Zohar? Well, once I was standing on the street in Woodstock, New York when a tourist approached me and asked, "Are you someone?"

Understanding she thought I was a celebrity because of my hair beard and attitude, "No" I answered "I just look like I'm someone."

1

Chapter Six

HOW TO READ ZOHAR

The autistic are known to have communication difficulties. I could not speak until three but no one could understand me until years later. At the end of her very long life, my mother said to me, No one could every understand you. Plus, I had this added difficulty, I am unable to remember sound. I lived in Israel for ten years; I am fluent in Hebrew—but, I couldn't understand a word anyone said. Eventually my inability to remember sound, drove me back to America. Yet, sometimes a disability is just what is needed.

Along with my inability to remember sound, I was always a very slow reader. Reading Zohar requires patience; it is incumbent on the reader to absorb the nuances of the words—beyond the simple meaning. Those relying on the sound of the words will miss the inner meaning disguised in the letters combined into words. These twenty-two phonetic letters correspond to the twenty-two movements of the mouth, to the ten aspects of the Tree of Life male and female, each with an essence. The first letter **א/Aleph-1** is male and the last letter **ת/Tof-400** is female, the other letters intertwine, blending gender together.

Learning the Hebrew alphabet is essential to understanding Zohar because both Hebrew and Aramaic are written using the same alphabet, which makes deciphering words tricky. Because the alphabet is phonetic, Hebrew, an ancient and beautiful language, is simple to learn, opening up all the ancient books. I have read the book of **תה־לים/Tihilim-Psalms** hundreds of times without understanding, just for the beautiful sound of the words; I have said the ancient prayer three times a day for fifty years for the same reason—a beautiful gift to the Creator. But, Torah is meant to be learned and understood, word by precious word.

Every word of Torah is a Name of God. Since all things sweet or harsh, come from the Creator; free choice is activated when choosing God—choosing to study Zohar is approaching the Creator from the highest point in creation, the Truth of the Truth. Each word engraved through and through with a knowledge meant for the eye and not for the ear. Hearing is an incremental apparatus but seeing encompasses everything at one moment. Zohar appeals to the eye, like a good novel; Zohar is able to transport the reader to a different realm where spiritual worlds teem—Zohar is amazing.

Zohar is not meant to be read as a book but rather a continuing conversation between Rebbe Shimmon and Moshe Shem Tov de Leon, a channeled work of about a million words. The source of Zohar can be traced back to the original manuscripts, there is no alternative text. Throughout Zohar, the Rabbis who accompany Rebbe Shimmon continually bemoan the idea that when Rebbe Shimmon leaves this world, his light will be gone. This was a way of reminding Rebbe Shimmon he had not written down his knowledge as had the other Rabbis of his time, this fourth level of Torah into a book.

Rebbe Shimmon knew his knowledge was inappropriate for his generation since the dusk of an illustrious thousand years of נצח/**Netzak-Victory** was transmuting into the thousand years of הוד/**Hod-Retreat**. Rome had destroyed the last vestige of the Jewish dream with the victory over Bar Chochva 120 years before the year four thousand. Later, Rome by their own calendar of calculations proclaimed two thousand with 240 years left until the year six thousand, signifying the end of Rome with the falling of the Trade Towers. Rome stole 120 years from Yisroel and paid back double on the other end. The final 240 years is the transition time from man to woman.

Zohar is meant for our dark time when all the truth in the world amounts to one big lie. The concept of Truth has become a bad joke.

People are reduced down to servitude, caught between the strictures of government based on science and the strictures of religion based on dogma. Zohar needs to be revealed in our time because the greatest light comes from the darkest darkness. For two thousand years, Onward Christian Soldier inspired war has ravished the world, now war is being extended into outer space with their new Space Force—but, the time of war is ending. There is no longer an appetite for war, anywhere in the world.

As a sign the darkness is ending, Zohar appears like the mighty orb glowing just beneath the approaching horizon. Society has the technology and equipment to verify the lucidity of Zohar in a cogent visual language easily understood by all. Zohar pierces the darkness of ignorance and stupidity; a little bit of light pushes away a lot of darkness—step by step, Zohar helps strip away the impurities of life, letting in the light. Zohar destroys the concept of monotheism by establishing the Creator to be completely beyond creation.

Once able to recognize the twenty-two Hebrew letters, the reader can commence to read without comprehension, just to follow the cadence of the words, giving emphasis to comas and periods. All ancient Hebrew text is meant to be said with a song and until the reader hears the humming of the song, the cognition of the words and the meaning of what is written will remain hidden. The mouth needs time, molding to turns and twists of each letter and word until the Hebrew becomes comfortable brushing against the lips. Taking words from Heaven and projecting then into the world can only bring blessing.

Reading awakens the mind's eye to remember the past. Going all the way back to the very beginning until the words of Zohar become common in the mouth and familiar to the ear. The Hebrew is quoted from the Torah but Aramaic is used in the narrative discussions spoken from high, translating what is in Heaven by means of a conversation on Earth with a Rabbi in Spain. Seven hundred years later, the time has come to delve into the depth of Zohar. The time has come to read Zohar.

LET'S READ ZOHAR

The word חרות/**Choret-Etched** can also be translated חרות/**Choret-Free**. The original words of the Torah were etched into the two cubes comprising the Ten Commandments; each shard from the engraving carved with the Finger of God was one of the twenty-two Hebrew letters which Moshe used to compose the Torah. The Torah is also known as Torat Emet/True Teaching. The first five books of the Torah are known as חומש/**Chomesh-Five**. Another nineteen Written Books of prophesy were added, along with the Oral Tradition committed to print two thousand years ago has grown exponentially.

The teaching of Truth along with the expectation of perfection is accomplished by a simple method: logic cannot contradict the Torah—the translation, explanation or extrapolation can never contradict what is written anywhere else in the twenty-four books of the Written Torah. Much of the Oral Torah is involved with settling seemingly contradictory events and ideas scattered throughout the Written Word. Plus, there are seventy faces to each aspect of Torah, so as long as ideas and impressions from the Torah do not contradict, then the idea belongs to one of the reflections from the seventy faces of Torah.

There is no dogma in the Torah; all views are of equal voracity—yet, Torah scholars are famous for their incessant arguments. These famous arguments between the Rabbis enshrined in the Talmud were for the sake of Heaven, meaning: They all agreed, each was correct in their view but would push each other to refine their thinking by pointing out seemingly contradictory ramifications of each idea which had to be defended to remain in the breath of Torah. Truth is not about right and wrong; Truth is not dogmatic—Truth is God's reality of creation. God creates creation moment by moment. We are the mirror reflecting back from the bottom of creation.

CHAPTER SEVEN

ZOHAR FROM THE BEGINNING

First Paragraph
בריש הורמנותא דמלכא, גליף גלופי בטהירו עלאה בוצינא
דקרדינותא, ונפיק גו סתים דסתימו מרזא דאין סוף, קוטרא בגולמא
נעיץ בעזקא לא חוור ולא אוכם ולא סומק ולא ירוק, ולא גוון כלל כד
מדיד משיחא עביד גוונין לאנהרא לגו. בגו בוצינא נפיק חד
נביעו, דמניה אצטבעו גוונין לתתא.

בריש הורמנותא דמלכא
In the Head of the High King

In any teaching, questions are a requisite. Questions show a lack of understanding; to a teacher, the question is an opportunity to impart knowledge into the empty vessel of the student—one who does not question does not learn. For example, the first three words of Book Zohar: הורמנותא דמלכא/**In the Head of the High King** is full of questions. This Aramaic phrase is tied to the first word in the ־ברא שת:תורה/**In the Beginning** illuminating a generality in the תורה, the oral explanation of the text can never be separated from the simple meaning of the written word.

The simple meaning is not the literal meaning, as in ברשאת/**In the Beginning**, in the beginning of what? The simple explanation is: In the beginning of these seven thousand years of human creation upon planet Earth. However, זהר adds a new dimension by referring to the beginning of creation, what scientists call the Big Bang, where something comes out of nothing. The illogic of something from nothing spawns other aberrant theories like life arising from the inanimate or human evolution from apes. What really happened? Nothing came out of something.

Before creation happened, the concept of nothing did not exist. All that existed was בורא/**Creator** and אור/Light of בורא/**Creator** known as **אור אין סוף/OreAinSof-LightWithoutEnd** a quiescent light considered, The Great Name of God. The עיץ חיים/**Tree of Life** is the geometric prototype to form made from ten luminaries with specific attributes stamped everywhere throughout creation, but the Great Name אור אין סוף/**OreAinSof-LightWithoutEnd** has infinite attributes. Just as a name is not the person, the Name of God is not God. The Creator is completely beyond Names. God is nothing of Heaven or Earth, therefore God can be everywhere to everyone always.

The letter ב/**Bet-2** begins both the Written תורה and זהר. The letter ב/**Bet-2** at the beginning of a word is generally a preposition meaning, In or With, combined with the word ראש/**Head**, together mean: **In the Head**. Elsewhere in זהר is written, Creation went up in the Mind of בורא/**Creator**. בורא has no head and no mind but these two similes correspond to the first two aspects of creation. The head is where the brain and mind are housed forming a confine. For בורא who is beyond any kind of confine, descending into the head is low. בורא wants to be known in low but a simple confine is not low enough to satisfy God's Desire which went up into the mind of בורא indicating creation would be based on logic, depicted as cause and effect. The next two words הורמנותא דמלכא/**Height of the King**, refers to the Tree of Life, the High King, meaning—the Tree of Life planted in the head, a confined area within the אור אין סוף/**LightWithoutEnd**. It is the עיץ חיים/**Tree of Life** which adds dimension to the confine bringing about high and low. High is in the brain and low is in the mouth. So why didn't the text say, High and Low instead of **High** and **King**?

The human being is formed in the precise image of the עיץ חיים/**Tree of Life** composed with ten attributes. Similarly, the Earth is formed from seven continents and three oceans and the solar system is made of the Sun and nine planets. The human form is comprised by these same ten attributes into three triangles: head, torso and arms, legs plus sex and lastly, mouth considered מלך/**King**, since the king rules by decree from the lips of the ruler. What separates the human being from the animal is our ability to articulate thoughts into words.

The עץ חיים/**Tree of Life** comes from the Name י-ה-ו-ה. The י-ה corresponds to the two hemispheres of the brain and ו/**Vav-6** corresponds to two lower triangles: torso and arms, hips and sex. The final Hey-ה/**5** is found in the power of speech. The י-ה-ו-ה reflects the concept of אחד/**One** since these four letters can be rearranged to make the three states of time: היה/**Past**; הוה/**Present**; יהי/**Future**. Time and space are encapsulated by this famous Four Letter Name י-ה-ו-ה. The אור אין סוף/**LightWithoutEnd** is composed of infinite Names. זהר begins by giving the coordinates to creation: a bubble composed of ten, floating within an infinity of light. בריש הורמנותא דמלכא/**In the Head High King** is the prototype to creation replicated in the production of stars into the galaxy, the form of the solar system, the form of the Earth and the form of the human being. בריש הורמנותא דמלכא/**In the Head High King** represents the primal beginning of creation establishing the עשר ספרות/**Ten Luminaries** etched with all the information necessary to conduct the entirety of creation from the high spiritual worlds down to תבל/**Earth**, the lowest place in creation.

גליף גלופי בטהירו עלאה בוצינא דקרדינותא

Completely Engraved in High Brightness the Cradle of Hardness

זהר describes the initial process of creation as an engraving, hollowing out in a spiral motion from within the אור אין סוף/**LightWithoutEnd** a place for creation to exist by means of attenuation causing weight to occur. Yet, at this level, the אור/**Light** and כלי/**Vessel** are one. The אור אין סוף/**LightWithoutEnd** has no end because there is no motion. The symbiotic relationship between time and space is measured in movement. The spinning motion of a tool hollowing out a space for creation happened by entering the smallest letter **י/10** just a point with a tiny horn caused the static energy to turn dynamic. The confine of time and space is low to בורא who is without confines yet wants to be known in low. Since בורא is beyond time and space בורא is able to create all possibilities from the very beginning. The end point of creation is the physical manifestation of עיץ חיים**/Tree of Life**. The human being walking upon תבל**/Earth** with בחירה חופשית**/B'Chira Chofshet-Free Choice** is the lowest level of creation. The first angel, מִיכָאֵל**/Michael** was created by בורא to have cognizance recognizing the Creator of שמים**/Ethereal** and ארץ**/Terrestrial**. Seemingly, the purpose of creation had been fulfilled בורא who is high was acknowledged by creation who is low, but the desire of בורא could not be satisfied by one angel. Like the unscratchable itch, creation forged further forward until the universe became cornucopia teeming with spiritual life, angels without end all replicated from the first angel מִיכָאֵל**/Michael**.

Everything in creation was set from this primordial engraving of the עיץ חיים into the space made within the אור אין סוף. There are ten components to the עיץ חיים and the number ten is connected to the letter **י** through gematria. The form of the letter **י** depicts the head of a drill, the first movement of creation eventually displayed in the universe based on ten: the Sun and nine planets, seven continents and three oceans and the human form built in three triangles plus the power of speech. The letter **י** is also engraved in the opening at the end of the penis, considered the source of nakedness, exposing the first letter of the Name י-ה-ו-ה.

The word דקרדינות contains two words depicting different aspects of hardness: קר**/Heavy** in Aramaic and דין**/Law** in Hebrew. Both Heavy and Law come from contraction. The קבלה**/Cabala**, key to זהר, calls this first action of creation צמצון הראשון**/Ztmzton HaRishon-First Contraction** vacating the original light, leaving a swirling space in place of the original light which had fled. The בוצינא**/Candlestick** gives the sense of metal hardness twisting within the אור אין סוף**/LightWithoutEnd** causing perturbations percolating out a disturbance within the quiescent nature of the Great Name.

בוצינא דקרדינו is what is on the far side of creation we call the BlackWhole. גליף גלופי/**Thoroughly Engraved** means, there were many BlackWholes within the first contraction called מוקם פוני/**Empty Space**. זהר gives us a glimpse into what occurred to create the BlackWholes and how they came to produce stars in a spiraled form like the initial engraving twisting through the אור אין סוף/**LightWithoutEnd**. Only in the last hundred years have telescopes been able to observe what Rebbe Shimmon explained in זהר. The universe has a logical construction; זהר presents a strong challenge to those who believe in a Big Bang Theory where something comes out of nothing for no reason—nihilism.

ונפיק גו סתים דסתימו מרזא דאין סוף

Went Out from Inside Most Hidden from a Hint of Infinity

Ten is a hint to infinity, a bubble of creation from where the desire of בורא to be known in low can be satisfied. The אור אין סוף/**LightWithoutEnd** is quiescent because there is no differential, all is equal, whereas creation is made from dynamic differentials values and systems. The concept of going out indicates space and therefore speed measured in time. If something is going out, the question arises, from where did something go out from? And what is going out? How is it possible the עץ חיים/**Tree of Life** can be transported through endless contractions and still remain intact?

There are those who want to say, if you put all of creation together, that is god, but from זהר we see that is ridiculous. Creation at the highest level is only a tiny bubble etched into the Great Name. Wherever we see בורא we see the humility of בורא willing to come down to our level and stand together with us, each one of us, whose story is beautiful before בורא who creates moment by moment all of creation accounting for the mystifying conundrum of physical movement.

The first contraction caused the separation between ten and infinity, but subsequent contractions happen from a logical basis called, cause and effect; as is known, בורא created and destroyed worlds until בורא got what was wanted—our universe with endless BlackWholes sporting unique galaxies throughout the universe. This is how chaos turned into order because fueling the chaos was the original inscription carved into the skull of creation beginning with perturbations causing BlackWholes producing hardness from where stars are destined to come forth. Once we see where creation is, then it is easier to understand our place within the scope of creation.

Within the parameters of the אור אין סוף/**LightWithoutEnd** there is no in or out, no up or down, no differential at all, perfect in quiescence until בורא had a desire capsulated within an insignificant bubble, like a tiny bubble in a swelling sea of endless water. Only the Will of בורא allows creation to exist. But, בורא is patient. Since time is part of being low, then בורא must wait for the satisfaction coming from being known in low.

Even בורא needs to obey the Laws of Creation for freedom of choice to to remain a choice.

קוטרא בגולמא נעיץ בעזקא לא חוור ולא אוכם ולא סומק ולא ירוק ולא גוון כלל

Form Inserted Into Amorphous Ring Not White And Not Black And Not Red And Not Green And No Color At All

The line of effluence coming forth from the hint of the אור אין סוף/**LightWithoutEnd** twisted into a spiral by the ring of בוצינא דקרדינותא/**Cradle of Hardness** creates the BlackWhole from where the stars are born in the form of a spiral swirling through space. The apparent chaos is not to be believed. The appearance of disorder we see from our standpoint on תבל embedded in a solar system situated far from the lips of a spewing BlackWhole is false. Facts contradict theories until scientists are baffled by the exactness of chaos as they grapple with the Truth. Science is continually changing while religion never changes; these are the two choices available to society—yet, neither is true.

Scientists wonder how a big bang could produce the same kind of atom everywhere throughout the universe? זהר answers, The ten components of the עיץ חיים/**Tree of Life** incubated within the letter י transforming into splintering shards evacuating the original **אור אין סוף/LightWithoutEnd** but leaving a hint in the form of **עיץ חיים/ Tree of Life**. A faint trace of what was initially the infinite Names of **בורא** reduced down into four letters: **י-ה-ו-ה** the everlasting seed to the **Tree of Life** imprinted throughout creation. Though something was happening, the absence of color indicated the absence of time, meaning: movement happened immediately at a speed far exceeding the speed of light. The sine wave had yet to manifest.

The definition of life is movement, if it moves it's alive. Scientists try to stop the movement of the atom by freezing the atom into submission but they are unable to reach absolute zero because without movement the atom would disappear and cease to exist. בורא has put a perimeter around creation in the form of the speed of light on one hand and absolute zero on the other hand, the right and left hands of בורא squeezing creation to produce life. The speed of light and absolute zero are the two boundaries of time and space.

Color indicates differential degrees and value. The frequency of color attenuated into an atom and eventually in coordination with other atoms produced a frequency in the form of a wavelength uniquely suited for each particular element. Scientists are able to identify the elements present in the furthest reaches of outer space by their color signature. However, scientific predictions are predicated on a skewed understanding that time is a line. Time spirals, like our galaxy and our DNA. Plotting a spiral is different than plotting a line which only produces a fake reality. Changing the way we understand time will change and improve the world when truth pervades both Heaven and Earth. The more in sync we move, the closer we come to בורא.

זהר explains how infinity slows down to the speed of light which has two opposite dispositions. The ray component of light wants to go faster but the material of light wants to expand to infinity where movement ends, causing light to go slower, thus a balance is struck between these two opposite expanses where matter and ray are woven together creating physical light where the infinite and the finite dance the dance of life. Death separates the physical body from the light of the soul.

כד מדיד משיחא עביד גוונין לאנהרא לגו

When Space Became Measurable Color Glowed Within

The attenuation of creation from the Oneness of בורא reflected in the אור אין סוף/LightWithoutEnd down to time and space is equivalent to nothing coming out of something. The תלמוד/Talmud describes creation coming about through two lines of light along one side of the loom commanded to go out and create. One line went in, which was male and the other line went out, which was female; since, this was a primordial form, actual man and woman are the opposite—man goes out and woman goes in. Then בורא said די/**Di-Enough** and creation stopped expanding. These two lines are the two components of light: ray and particle.

One of the seven Hebrew names of בורא is שדי/**Shadai-Who Said** די/**Di-Enough** to the expansion of creation. The gematria of שדי is **314** the first three numbers of pi, the interloper between the line and the curve. When בורא gave the command to creation to stop, the line of light halted and became a point which then reverberated back turning into waves, what scientists call the background noise from creation. Science and תורה need not contradict. The facts of science corroborated by ancient wisdom should work in tandem. The structure of creation is essential to know that our world belongs to the Creator.

Looking at creation as though something came out of nothing is inacurate when, from God's point of view, nothing came out of something. Space time and color collude in tricking the human mind into thinking life happens spontaneously instead of a well thought out plan from בורא/**Creator** of the world. What science sees is from outside the BlackWhole but זהר confers from within the BlackWhole, a cogent understanding inferring how creation comes into being.

בגו בוצינא נפיק חד נביעו דמניה אצטבעו גוונין לתתא
Inside Hardness Went Out One Stream Coloring Below

The אור אחד/**One Light** brakes down endlessly into different vibrations indicative of various colors in the prism of creation passing through and giving birth to plurality; stemming from duality originated by the initial separation between אור אין סוף/**LightWithoutEnd** reduced down to ten creating a universe with endless multiplicity intertwining matter and ray bringing about life on planet תבל/**Earth**—a place able to sustain billions of human beings free to articulate thoughts into speech. The initial vibration of creation is the voice of בורא. In creation, only בורא and the human being speak; בורא commands and we respond—according to the limits of our freewill.

בורא weaves together color to make creation. Each person is enlivened by a line of light connected to their soul having been engraved out of a star. For a short period of time in this physical world we are able to wheel our light upon תבל and in doing so, change all of creation by adding a unique thread into the loom embroidered with Heaven and Earth. Not only did בורא create creation but בורא continues to create creation because one moment without the Creator creating, creation ends forever. בורא is here for all us all the time everywhere throughout creation.

The בוצינא/**Candlestick** is how the BlackWhole looks from the inside surrounded by אור אין סוף/**LightWithoutEnd**. This original contraction creating an aperture where within the friction of contraction caused the coalescing of weight eventually causing an outburst of effluence into an ejaculation of celestial perturbations expressed as endless נקודה/**Nikuda-BlackWhole** each with an effluence of elements destined to become stars and planets. Thus the universe was born.

The speed of light is the innate confine to movement, stopping creation from further expansion. Yet, baffled scientists insist the universe is speeding up into empty space and are unable to supply a reason. What is pushing the universe to expand? According to זהר everything is running towards the אור אין סוף/LightWithoutEnd which surrounds creation and everything within creation. Atrophy is not the end of creation, unity is the finality of creation after eons of years. There is no limit as to how high we can go. Unity below, connects with the unity above.

Space will eventually be swallowed up and time will disappear in a celestial burp but what we have done, good and bad, will forever be part of the perfect weave in the אור אין סוף the Great Name of בורא. Nonetheless, בורא is completely beyond time and space and nothing we can do will affect בורא but the Great Name of בורא will be changed by our actions, particularly on this low level of existence where a physical cloak hides the light, producing free choice. All the wonders of the universe are orchestrated only for the sake of our world, the center of creation.

Paragraph Two
סתים גו סתימין מרזא דאין סוף, בקע ולא בקע, אוירא דיליה לא אתיידע כלל. עד דמגו דחיקו דבקיעותיה, נהיר נקודה חדא סתימא עלאה, בתר ההיא נקודה לא אתיידע כלל, ובגין כך אקרי ראשית מאמר קדמאה דכלא.

סתים גו סתימין מרזא דאין סוף בקע ולא בקע אוירא דיליה
לא אתיידע כלל
Hidden Within Hidden From Hint of AinSof/ WithoutEnd Out but Not Out Space is Completely Unknown.

The inside of the נקודה/Nikuda-Dot (Blackwhole) is radiant from the energy of movement without motion causing interaction based on possibilities, bringing about a contraction, opening a space where there was no space. There is no way to accurately say what goes on within the non-reflective nature of the נקודה but the great weight within the נקודה portends to the fomenting of creation prior to time and space. Everything destined to be was in potential within the נקודה inscribed with the Desire of בורא to be known in low. Every particular in creation is rooted in the original נקודה the letter י/Yud-10.

זהר helps the human mind bridge the divide between creation and בורא the Creator. Through an intricate description of what occurred prior to creation, motivated by a desire gone up in the Mind of God to be known in low, a basic understanding of what occurred can be gleamed. The ramifications of this Supernal Thought put into action an immediate result, creation of time and space within the אור אין סוף accomplished within the confines of logic to produce our universe. Using the confines of logic בורא is able to fashion creation as an intermediary between God and the human being able to articulate thoughts into words in much the same way בורא articulates creation into existence.

עד דמגו דחיקו דבקיעותיה נהיר נקודה חדא סתימא עלאה

Until Because Friction Within Shone Unique Illuminated Dot Hidden Above

From the side of creation, this dark point is a massive נקודה/Nikuda-Dot giving birth to a universe of stars engraved with a form, depicting the עיץ חיים made out of ten constituent parts. Perfection has no friction, no contradiction, no opposite mirrored interaction, no duality at all, just perfect interconnections tether to the Emanator of Light, in the same way each ray of sunlight is connected to the sun. The Desire of בורא keeps creation created. Moment by moment בורא creates creation creating each atom slightly moved. The Creator is constantly tinkering with the fabric of creation.

Every aspect of creation connects back to the original Desire of בורא to be known in low. Every action, indeed every thought and word uttered since the beginning of human occupation upon planet תבל is reflected back to בורא through the web of spiritual worlds, eventually sucked into the נקודה and transmitted back to the source of creation in a feeble attempt to satisfy the Supernal Longing. Desire is beyond logic. בורא is facing each person who reflects back according to free will; everything between is the intermediary able to convey sustained communication between high and low—between בורא and the human being, called אדם/**Adom-One Blood.**

Prior to creation, there was no high and low, light and darkness; movement was like sexual union where there is no space between the two genders—primordial creation is androgynous. Sexual metaphors pervade the Torah because sex is the language of life when two dualities momentarily become one. בורא adopts the rules of creation to accomplish a real understanding of the receiver. בורא is usually referred to as male since the Creator gives while creation receives. This disparity between these two disparate realities is dark on one side and light on the other side while the bubble of desire separates between.

זהר begins by rendering a description as to how נקודה/**Nikuda-Dot** came into existence, a funnel through which the stars would be born. This information prior to the invention of the telescope was useless. Zohar was just a bright light blinding whoever looked within the pages, whose own words predict זהר would be needed and understood at the End of Days at the advent to the Thousand Years of Woman and Peace. זהר accomplishes this by describing creation validated by science. Physical fact combined with spiritual method plus the intention of the Creator in creation unify within the words of זהר.

בתר ההיא נקודה לא אתידע כלל ובגין כך אקרי ראשית
מאמר קדמאה דכלא

Beyond This Dot Nothing is Known Therefore Called, ראשית/Beginning the First Word To Everything

זהר depicts creation from two sides of the original נקודה/**Dot** wherein creation exists. This dot is beyond time and space yet to be created.

The inside of the נקודה is illuminated but on the outside is a Black-Whole from where the universe shoots out a spiraled ejaculation of stars. Each star is a shard from the original engraving and each soul is carved from a star shinning down upon the planet תבל attaching to a body coming closer to God through means of free choice.

זהר written two thousand years ago explains what scientists describe in their feeble attempt to break the code of creation. The importance of זהר in our time is to throw spiritual light upon the shadow of belief. Belief is what we do not know, if we knew, we would have no reason to believe. All of creation is fitted inside this נקודה the dot of the BlackWhole with darkness on one side and light on the far side, a light beyond any conjecture, an unknown light called: זהר corroborated by scientific fact while correcting speculation.

From our station upon planet תבל our galaxy is enormous; but, when looking further into the universe we find an endless array of other galaxies and worlds extending close to 14 billion light years away—but, time is an assumption based on the speed of light. From the moment אור/**Light** ejaculated into the spaceless space, אור was untethered from speed. Only after being commanded by בורא to halt creating, as the Talmud describes בורא yelling at creation **Di/Enough** until creation stopped thus creating the Name שדי/**Shadai-Who Said** די/**Enough**.

Once creation came to a standstill, then the reverberations from the sudden stop caused light to slow, refracting back at the speed of light, considered by the ancients as ליכה/**Walking**. The ancients measured the distance in Heaven as, five hundred years walking between the spaces in space. Since planet תבל is the center of creation, where the human being practices freedom of choice, the secret of time is hidden in planet תבל. The 365 day year squared times the two thousand years the Creator played with creation equals 266,450,000 years, the amount of time needed to come forth from the BlackWhole until stopped.

Scientists say, it took about a quarter of million years for the stars to blink on but the תורה is more exact. Also, the number 26645 answers the ancient question, Why בורא began the creation of our seven thousand year cycle here on planet תבל 5780 years ago is because 26 is the gematria of God's Name and 45 isthe gematria of **אדם/Adom-Human Being** and the 6 in between are the Six Days of Creation prototype to the six thousand year calendar concluding with the Thousand Years of Woman and Peace in 220 years. The purpose of creation is for the human being to know the Creator through the Six Days of Creation.

Paragraph Three

והמשכילים יזהירו כזהר הרקיע ומצדיקי הרבים ככוכבים לעולם ועד. זהר סתימא דסתימין, בטש אוירא דיליה ואנהיר האי נקודה, וכדין אתפשט האי ראשית, ועביד היכלא ליקריה, ולתושבחתיה. תמן זרעא דקודשא לאולדא לתועלתא דעלמא ורזא דא זרע קדש מצבתה.

והמשכילים יזהירו כזהר הרקיע ומצדיקי הרבים ככוכבים לעולם ועד

The Knowledge Transmitters Glow Like Brilliance in The Heavens And Disperse Great Merit Like Stars To The World Forever

The knowledge of creation was known from the very beginning but has been necessarily diminished for dissemination throughout the world. Throughout the ages knowledge has accrued until our time when Truth is hidden beneath a veneer of fake news operating on faulty assumptions fueled by dogmatic ideas. This is when the illumination contained in זהר is unleashed to proclaim from the stars: the randomness of creation is an illusion. The Truth is found in structure, where there is structure, there is Truth.

Holding the thread of this knowledge connects the person to the source of Truth, the Creator בורא who is neither physical nor spiritual, who is unencumbered by space and time or any other obstruction. בורא sees everything but waits to tell. בורא creates a puzzle sprinkled with hints along pathways supporting all peoples going in all directions.

Beauty and Truth are in the heart of each human being. Each person wants, in their essence, to get close to the Creator בורא. Some run straight to the light while others prefer to take a step back before going forward.

All directions in life are supported by the Creator fueled by love, but there are rules. Without recognizing these rules of restraint, the person is lost in man-made paths going nowhere, obscuring the Truth. Those able to convey this inner knowledge throughout the generations have given the world a tether to בורא in the form of the עץ חיים with 613 roots threading through the inner workings of the universe, segmented into the body of our solar system then divided into seven segments: head (Sun, Mercury Venus); right arm (Earth); left arm (Mars); torso (Jupiter); right leg (Saturn); left leg (Uranus); sex (Neptune); speech (Pluto). Similarly, There are Seven Commandments to all Peoples and there are 613 Commandments to the Jewish People who are the Chosen People, chosen to perform the 613 Commandments, the wind to the world.

Science continually changes but אמת/Truth never changes, yet אמת goes on forever. Those great thinkers who preserved this ancient knowledge did so by word of mouth. Nothing was written down, only hinted at in other writings. The small cadre of mystical Rabbis quoted often throughout the text of זהר remind Rebbe Shimmon that when he leaves this world his light will be sorely missed, a subtle way of begging him to write his brilliance into words, but he refused. The זהר ends with Rebbe Shimmon's death while his closest comrade Rav Aba says, I am standing here pen in hand but Rebbe Shimmon's refuses to commit his knowledge into writing.

זהר is too powerful to be written into the corporeal, only in שמים could זהר be written then transmitted through conversation in Aramaic which softens the complexity written into the original text carved into the firmament of שמים. The celestial conversation with Moshe Shem Tov de Leon was a way of attenuating the brightness of זהר accompanied by the recitation of conversations two thousand years ago on this world which are also engraved in שמים. Even with all that, it took a thousand years to be revealed in this dark and needy time of human tribulation.

זהר סתימא דסתימין בטש אוירא דיליה ואנהיר האי נקודה
Hidden Brilliance Pushed Space illuminating the Dot

The word זהר is used to indicate the inner sanctum of the נקודה/**Dot**. The BlackWhole is where the accumulating sparks of אור/**Light** made from the original engraving into the אור אין סוף/**OreAinSof** coalesced together creating weight through the contours of endless contractions. The circular movement from the original engraving caused זהר to funnel down into נקודה/**Dot** pushing out to create space and illumination streaming forth from the BlackWhole, נקודה/**Dot**.

זהר is the most hidden of all Jewish teachings, depicting the inner parts of the BlackWhole from where creation percolates out from a metal hardness down to a point from where ejaculation into an open space occurs. זהר breaks creation down into four parts called: עבי"א/**ABYA**: אצילות/**Atzilut-Close**; בריא/**Briah-Creation**; יצירה/**Yitzirah-Form**; עשיה/**Asyia-Action**, seen from תבל as: solar system, galaxy, BlackWhole and זהר/**Brilliance** from the far side of the BlackWhole—further depicted by the soul made also in four parts: נפש/**Nefesh-Movement**; ראח/**Ruach-Spirit**; נשמה/**Neshema-Breath**; כתר/**Keter-Crown**. All based from The Name י-ה-ו-ה.

The illumination birthed by the BlackWhole is a stream of energy quickly condensing down into elements, exploring the outer reaches where the confines of space merge back into the אור אין סוף causing the rest of creation to continuously speed up, coming closer to the Source. Merging back is the ultimate goal that will never be reached since בורא will continually want a Dwelling Place in Low. The angels play out this balancing act of opposite desires in a movement called: רצה ושוב/**Rutzi V'Shaav-Running and Returning**. The Creator בורא wants to get lower while creation wants to get higher. The continuing goal is to meet in the middle with a big hug.

וכדין אתפשט האי ראשית ועביד היכלא ליקריה ולתוש־
בחתיה

In Order to Expand This Beginning and Make Magnificent Chambers For Praise

The effluence of the stars pushed out from the BlackWhole created divisions, yet left the threads of interconnectedness spliced together throughout the universe. Chambers are continually created where the angels do their work amid places for souls to hang out awaiting descension down to תבל. Scientists sense these chambers, defying measurement. Scientists call them, Dark Matter along with Dark Energy making up 96 percent of the universe. We are only able to detect four percent of the whole, contained in the four elements.

Scientists wonder at the conformity within the universe, how each atom is precisely the same as every other atom even though the logic of the Big Bang Theory dictates the opposite. If indeed, chaos was the progenitor of the universe then reality would be truly subjective. Structure indicates logic; creation is logical, based on cause and effect—nature is logical. However, cause and effect cannot produce structure and certainly cannot produce life. Only the Creator בורא creates life in a structured universe compelled by הטבע/HaTeva-The Nature with the gematria of 86 the same as the Name אלהים/Elohim-God governing plurality. These two Names, י-ה-ו-ה and אלהים are Father and Mother to Creation, the fundamental way Creator experiences gender.

The desire of בורא to be known in low is engraved into the Great Name causing a BlackWhole to open up into a universe of BlackWholes each sprouting a galaxy. בורא chose the Milky Way Galaxy to be home to the initial desire propelling creation upon planet תבל where all the stars in the heavens are tethered to our solar system constantly feeding our world life through a complex weave of light within a myriad of chambers carved into the heavens attenuating the Light זהר down to illumination. זהר illuminates creation for the Creator בורא to be acknowledged and praised.

תמן זרעא דקודשא לאולדא לתועלתא דעלמא ורזא דא זרע
קדש מצבתה

There an Independent Seed of Conception To Elevate World And Hints at Indestructible Independent Seed

The germination of the עיץ חיים/**Tree of Life** planted in the primordial BlackWhole growing down is infusing energy everywhere. תבל is furthest from the light; everything else in creation has greater cognition of בורא than does the human being here at lowest point in creation where בורא wants to be known in low. Life is rampant throughout the universe but there are no aliens evolving out of the leftovers precipitated from a Big Bang wielding something out of nothing. Everyone knows, nothing comes out of nothing.

The meticulous nature of creation is grown from the עיץ חיים/**Tree of Life** whose flowers give fruit upon the ground our world תבל. All life comes from that seed. The first human being was gathered from the dust of תבל so anywhere his progeny dies, the soil will accept the body back. A bit of the soul remains from each life hidden within a splinter of bone; a seed to a new body grown from the ground at the End of Days—a body impervious to pain, able to live for a thousand years.

The word מצבתה refers to a **Gravestone**, in Hebrew ז׳יון/**Zion-Hard**, rock of ages. The lifeline of light is incorruptible and will never stop pulsing through creation directed towards our world תבל appearing to circle the North Star every 26,000 thousand years in a galaxy whose center is 26,000 light years from the Earth which pulses every 26 seconds. The gematria of י-ה-ו-ה is 26. Half of 26 is 13 which is the gematria of אחד/**Echud-One**. There are two Ones in creation, the top and the bottom, all else is for conveyance, only. On That day God and God's Name will be One—בורא/**Creator**.

There are 600,000 letters in the תורה and each word is a Name of God. The Name is the closest we can come to God. We are all carved out from the Name, part of the Great Name אור אין סוף. Each person harbors that Holy Seed grown in the soil of our thoughts, watered by emotions until giving fruit through our actions which are often combined together in modules with hierarchies to administer the collective power. As in שמים/**Heaven** so it is on תבל/**Earth**. We are all grown from one seed to be one with י-ה-ו-ה.

Paragraph Four

זהר, דזרע זרע ליקריה, כהאי זרעא דמשי דארגוון טב, דאתהחפי לגו, ועביד ליה היכלא דאיהו תושבחתא דיליה ותועלתא דכלא. בהאי ראשית, ברא ההוא סתימא דלא אתיידע להיכלא דא. היכלא דא אקרי אלהים

זהר דזרע זרע ליקריה כהאי זרעא דמשי דארגוון טב דאתהח־
פי לגו

Illuminating the Seed Of Heaviness Like Persian Silk Tree With Abundant Color Covering Essence

The swirling light within the נקדה/**Dot** forms a seed of heaviness like the seed from the Silk Plant which is extremely red. The Persian Silk Tree is known for silky pink shoots. The unified light harboring within the נקדה/**Dot** was stretched out into one long lightwave measuring the expanse of space. Red is the sign of the first and longest lightwaves contracted down to the speed of light.

From the entanglement of tendrils was created chambers within the empty space of creation. Scientists are able to determine that the universe is speeding up because of the increase in redshifted light from the distant galaxies. The longer the wave, the speedier the object. Time spirals, therefore the beginning is red drawing through green then ending in blue. The sine wave does not infer conclusion just attenuation down to nothing since time is plotted as a line instead of a circle. This skewing of Truth has endless ramifications since motion measured by time is fundamental to existence.

However, from inside of the נקדה/**Dot** the slowing of light causes a blue shift. The עץ חיים/**Tree of Life** is set upon three pillars: right, left and center. Blue is the right, red is the left and center is green. The light of creation is said to be green, meaning light slowed down enough to allow creation to happen. Though the speed of light seems fantastically fast from our perspective but to בורא light is comparable to water slowly meandering through creation. Scientists are only able to see four percent of creation by their own admission.

Where there is a tree, first a seed needs to be. What happens within the BlackWhole is how this most ephemeral form of a seed was produced then planted into the מוקם פני/**Mokem Ponoi-Empty Space** sprouting the עיץ חיים rooted in שמים with branches spreading throughout the universe. Animals are considered temporal like the plants but the human being is compared to a tree deeply rooted in the ground. Animals go on all four, constantly staring at the dirt while human beings, a combination of human soul and animal body go erect with our heads elevated into the heavens.

ועביד ליה היכלא דאיהו תושבחתא דיליה ותועלתא דכלא
Making Her Chamber Praised While Elevating Everything

The difficulty in creation is restraining the infinite abilities of בורא down to the ten components of the עיץ חיים/**Tree of Life** engraved into the אור אין סוף/**LightWithoutEnd** creating a perturbation forming a seed within a miraculous chamber composing everything needed for creation to be replicated endlessly, culminating by feeding life into our planet תבל for human consumption. This supernal chamber is far beyond physical or spiritual, this chamber is the first appearance of form.

Coming from one seed, ensures uniformity throughout creation. All of creation can trace back to the original נקדה/**Dot** where בורא desires a dwelling place in low. From this point came many points until the universe was shaken by BlackWholes spewing out mammoth galaxies; each galaxy is a unique structure like none else—each a snowflake in the Eyes of בורא. A recognition of structure facilitates the notion that the Creator ברא created creation. The universe and all the life within the universe did not just happen but was planned from the very beginning. Even before time and space emerged, the seed to creation was already being formed within the initial BlackWhole.

The universe is completely unified, having sprouted from the same seed. Whatever there is in creation, belongs there; some for positive and some for negative—the job for each human being, here on the lowest place in creation with our head in the heavens and our feet upon the ground is to continually chose good over bad. We are not here just to satisfy our urges. There is a greater reason to life than our animal instincts. By seeding the heavens filled with hints illuminated by the great logic of creation only ברא could have created, the human being is faced with an existential decision to know God. The recognition between Creator ברא and creation exemplifies God being known by each person.

בהאי ראשית ברא ההוא סתימא דלא אתיידע
להיכלא דא היכלא דא אקרי אלהים

**This Beginning Creating The Hidden Unknowable
To This Chamber This Chamber Is Called Elohim**

The נקדה/**Dot** of the BlackWhole is counted as the beginning of creation when the red light from the inner blue seed spreads throughout space awakening the universe to the Creator ברא. We cannot know beyond the BlackWhole because that is the fifth dimension of creation, compared to the soul of the body. Just as the human being can only sense the soul, so too, the entire universe can only sense what is beyond the BlackWhole. זהר comes to teach about the light from the far side of the BlackWhole where God's Desire whirls and spins into a fecund gush of creation.

The BlackWhole begins time and space governed by the Name אלהים/**Elohim** which has a gematria of 86 the same gematria as טבע/**Teva-Nature** plus the five elementals: earth, water, air, fire and soul portrayed in the five letters אלהים/**Elohim**. The feminine attribution within creation is expressed through the Name אלהים/**Elohim** which is the combination of a few words and concepts. אל/**El-Kindness** is a Name indicating giving. By adding the letter ה/**Hey-5** which corresponds to the mouth breaking up the singularity of one breath into the multiplicity of speech through the five attributes of: throat, pallet, tongue, teeth and lips and is depicted in our solar system's most outer planet, Pluto with her five moons.

The word אלוה/**Eloha** translates as God and the final two letters ים adds plurality and renders the word ים/**Yaam-Sea** giving the final component to the Name אלהים/**Elohim**—the Name governing the multiplicity of creation. The Torah begins, בראשית ברא אלהים/**Bereshith Bora Elohim-In the Beginning Elohim Created** as if she is the birth Mother to creation. Later, the Name י-ה-ו-ה with a masculine influence becomes Father to creation. Because בורא/**Creator** is nothing of creation, בורא requires masculine and feminine Names enabling compassion for creation. Through the Names, בורא can be effected, feeling what creation feels.

בורא wants to be known in low and therefore, though בורא is everywhere all the time to everyone, nonetheless God wants to participate in creation, so בורא needs to adopt the restraints implicit to creation. בורא who is above time needs to have patience; בורא who loves justice needs to understand redemption— בורא who loves all of creation needs to be a good parent through the Names י-ה-ו-ה and אלהים. Though these Names come about at the brink of creation, the Name is not God. The Name is close to בורא but the Name is not בורא. We pray to בורא not to the Name of God.

Paragraph Five

ורזא דא, בראשית ברא אלהים. זהר, דמניה כלהו מאמרות אבריאו ברזא דאתפשטותא דנקודה דזהר סתים דא. אי בהאי כתיב ברא לית תווהא דכתיב ויברא אלהים את האדם בצלמו.

ורזא דא בראשית ברא אלהים

This Hint In The Beginning Elohim Created

The Written Torah begins with a description of the Six Days of Creation, beginning the six thousand year calendar embedded within the 266,450,000 years connecting the red light coming from the BlackWhole where within זהר is wrapped in blue filaments, a seed readied to be exploded out having been engraved into the אור אין סוף/LightWithoutEnd by the twisting Desire of בורא/Creator to be known in low.

The word בראשית can be rearranged to spell תשרי 'בא/**First Day of Tishri**. The New Moon in the month called Tishri is the sixth day of creation when the human being was formed. ראש השנה/**Rosh Ha-Shana-Head of the Year** begins a new cycle in the six thousand year calendar leading to the Thousand Years of Woman and Peace in 220 years. The first three words בראשית ברא אלהים/**In the Beginning God Created** hints to זהר the inner illumination of the primordial BlackWhole creating the beginning of time.

Embedded in time are the Six Thousand Years of Creation here on planet תבל happening after God-26 and Human Being-45 connect through the Six Days of Creation, after)26(6)45(000 years. Each of the Six Days of Creation is a prototype to a subsequent thousand years of history leading to the final Thousand Years of Woman and Peace. Presently, we are in the last quarter of the Sixth Day of Creation when the human being is created to stand erect with head in שמים and feet upon תבל harboring the freedom to chose a path through life coming towards culmination.

זהר דמניה כלהו מאמרות אבריאו ברזא דאונעששוונא
דנקודה דזהר סתים

Zohar From There Everything Spoken by Creator Hinted The Outflowing Dot Of Zohar Hidden

Out of זהר hidden within the BlackWhole, the Ten Utterances or waves of differentiation ordering the universe hinted in the form from עץ חיים/**Tree of Life** comprised of roots, trunk, branches and fruit growing down into creation. The עץ חיים rooted in the heart of creation is expressed in the oneness of the trunk branching out creating time and space where flowers come to fruition and sweetness grows on our corporeal Earth. זהר is just a reflection of a refraction percolating up form the essence endlessly attenuated down to the ground.

The first sound of creation, as taught in ספר יצירה/**Book of Form** written by Avraham four thousand years ago teaches, אמש/**Emesh**, a combination of three letters א-מ-ש, corresponding to: אביר/**air**; מים/**water**; אש/**fire**; the elements composing שמים/**Heaven**. The element of אבק/**Dust** is missing. Spiritual worlds void of corporeality are scattered throughout creation; clumps forming chambers in what the scientists describe as Dark Matter—unable to be breached by measurement. Scientists and philosophers lift their heads to the heavens wondering if there is life beyond Earth, while the entire universe of souls, angels, entities and other celestial vibrations laugh back at us.

Each person is etched from the planet **תבל**, a little pile of walking dirt but **בורא** sees things differently; **בורא** sees the hole left in the ground, sees the person as a walking hole which needs to be filled with the water of wisdom least noxious animals arise. Through our meandering upon the planet **תבל** through good deeds we do, filling our little walking hole with water to be an overflowing spring to our brethren. The moisture of life begins to dry as we age; some evaporate into stupidity, some pay the price of pleasure—but, the good we do replenishes the Good Earth like rain from the heavens.

זהר is etched from the inside of the BlackWhole, womb to existence and to our universe made of galaxies, revealed at this time סוף ימין/**End of Days** to help humanity out from the empty pit of darkness and the superficiality of modern day technology, fitting reality into a narrow screen for optimal consumption. We are the mirror of creation and what we do and what we express while on this planet reflects back even further than the place of emanation. זהר could only be revealed at this time when telescopes can corroborate the existence of black holes, where within זהר dwells.

אי בהאי כתיב ברא לית תווהא דכתיב ויברא אלהים את האדם בצלמו

With This Written ברא/Created No Wonderment is Written God ברא/Created Adom in God's Image

בורא who is neither physical nor spiritual certainly has no form. בורא experiences creation through Names and structures based in the ten components to the עיץ חיים. Only by seeing this structure implicit in the very first nascent beginnings to creation, can the human design and structure of creation be fully appreciated beyond art and science. Instead of staring out into the emptiness of man's ego and authority, זהר illuminates the עיץ חיים grown into our galaxy then reflected in our solar system as the Sun and nine planets mirrored on the Earth as three oceans and seven continents also depicted in the human con-figuration composed of ten components portrayed in three triangles plus speech. Seeing the thread of form drawn throughout dimen-sions expressing the essence of ten in various ways at different times conducted by the seven outer planets of our solar system and the myriads of stars beyond—is miraculous.

Both the body and the soul have form. The soul is carved from a star, tethered to a human body through a tiny beam of light entering into the right side of the brain initiating thinking, filling the body with endless abilities etched into the mind, the heart and the limbs bring-ing about thoughts, emotions and expression. If written vertical, the Name י-ה-ו-ה appears to be a stick figure of a human being. Each human being is born into the form of the י-ה-ו-ה each human being is tied to the illuminations of the soul—each person is a mirror re-flecting back.

The first אדם/**Adom** was formed androgynous connected male and fe-male back to back made from the dust of the Earth but the man was unable to see the woman, so בורא split the אדם/**Adom-One Blood** into two genders, able to explore each other's uniqueness. To בורא all of creation, physical and spiritual, is like one woman and בורא is her man. בורא is forever giving love into the relationship between Creator and creation. בורא adopts the endemic sexual language of nature to interact with creation. How else can בורא be known in low? Whatever the human being can imagine, בורא wants to be there experiencing life through each person all the time always.

Paragraph Six

זהר, רזא דא בראשית, קדמאה דכלא שמיה, אהיה, שמה קדישא גליפא בסטרוי, אלהים גליפא בעיטרא, אש"ר היכלא טמיר וגנין שריאותא דרזא דראשית אשר, ראש דנפיק מראשית.

זהר רזא דא בראשית קדמאה דכלא שמיה אהיה שמה קדישא גליפא בסטרוי

Zohar Hints At In The Beginning Prior To All Names אהיה Separate Name Engraved Within Hidden

The Name אהיה/**Eheya-To Be** is separate from all other subsequent Names. Engraved within זהר the inner dimension of the BlackWhole hinted in the first word of the Torah בראשית/**In The Beginning**. The Name אהיה/**Eheha-To Be** is completely hidden. The Name אהיה/**To Be** is the first Name after the initial engraving from the God's Desire to be known in low, depicting the ten components to the Tree of Life male and female each with an essence portrayed in the 22 letters of the ancient Hebrew alphabet. The letter א/**Aleph** is the first Hebrew letter, considered a general letter from where all other letters are born. א/**Aleph** spelled backwards is פלה/**Pelah-Wonderous**. The Name אהיה/**To Be** is considered a Name for the future.

God Spoke and the world was. Speaking begins in the head with a thought then is transmitted to the emotions taking on personality before being spit out into the world as a word. Similarly בורא adopts the ways of the world to intercourse with creation, beginning with a thought percolating from a Desire engraved into Endless Possibilities contracted down into a whirlpool of primordial light eventually merging into the first letter of creation, the letter **א/Aleph-1**. The iconic form of **א** depicts a diagonal line separating one dot into two dots on each side of a line, in the same way the BlackWhole separates in from out. The lower dot of the **א** is the outer dimension of the BlackWhole housing the universe.

From this first letter **א** in the Name אהיה propagates the next three letters to make **היה/Hoya-Past** which through gematria renders the number twenty which is equated with **כתר/Keter-Crown** also with a gematria of twenty. By surrounding the head, the entire body is surrounded; this is the essence expressed as Will and Pleasure—this is the gateway to the soul. However **כתר/Keter-Crown** without a body becomes an insatiable appetite for more, a shell sucking life from others. The Crown is the first revelation, an attribute refracted endlessly through creation, the essence of life reduced down to Will and Pleasure.

Will and Pleasure begins each pregnancy. The כתר of creation is seen in the BlackWhole, the first form of revelation from God's Will for the sake of God's Pleasure initiated by God's Desire. From the perspective of בורא future has already happened in infinite different ways all at once. The paths to each individual has already been forged, the choice is, which path to pursue? The **כתר/Keter-Crown** of the **מלך/Melech-King** are the first revelations to the power of Royalty. Similarly, the BlackWhole is just a tiny revelation compared to what hides within the BlackWhole, the light called **זהר/Brilliance**.

אלהים גליפא בעיטרא אשר היכלא טמיר וגנין שריאותא
דרזא דראשית אשר ראש דנפיק מן אשיוון

Elohim Engraved Into This Surrounding Hiding Chamber and Protecting the Beginning Hinted In ראשית/Beginning אשר/Preposition ראש/Head Comes Out From ראשית/Beginning

The Name אלהים/**Elohim** is a feminine Name indicating contraction and judgment; procuring the necessary elements needed to construct the universe—an ability bequeath to woman able to thread together a baby. Just as בורא engraves into the אור אין סוף/**LightWithoutEnd** so too, the Name אלהים is engraved into the rim of a newly opened space, giving birth to nature. Literally, the Name אלהים means, **God of Plurality**. Therefore, creation comes from כתר/**Keter-Crown** the BlackWhole where אלהים/**Elohim** is engraved into the hardness causing shards racing out into endless possibilities. Until creation was stopped by the Creator who shouted the word די/**Di-Enough** into creation, thus the Name שדי/**Shadi-Who Said** די-**Enough** with the gematria of 314 the first three digits of pi, interloper between the line and the curve, creation was unlimited.

The Aramaic word עיטרא/**Crown** refers to outside of the BlackWhole from where the universe opens, called ראשית/**Beginning** is a product of the Inner Chamber denoted by the word אשר/**Preposition** guarding from exposure from the first perturbation of Desire from בורא engraved into the אור אין סוף/**LightWithoutEnd** hinted in the word אשר/**Preposition**. The ראש/**Head** emerges first from the ראשית/**Beginning**. The BlackWhole produces an attenuated light drawn through the Name אלהים/**Elohim** breaking the OneLight into infinite beams going out into מוקם פני/**Mokim Panoi-Empty Space** creating chambers for the angels who are messengers from God.

The whole apparatus of שמים/**Heaven** is infinitely complex and confusing but that only extends to the BlackWhole. The Earth תבל one of nine planets in our solar system, is on an outer arm of our galaxy, full of endless stars all tethered to the BlackWhole which is the outer expression from the inner Will of בורא to fulfill a Godly Desire. Four thousand years ago Avraham came to this world from the Tower of Babel built on Mars to discover people on Earth who thought בורא had created creation then left the workings of creation in the hands of the planets and constellations.

Avraham came to our world with the message, בורא is One; meaning, One in the midst of plurality is everywhere to everyone all the time. True, בורא created the world through an unimaginable web of interaction from the most ephemeral of beginnings separating בורא/**Creator** from creation through the intercession of the BlackWhole, but בורא is not obstructed in anyway, whatsoever. בורא loves creation created through the Names of בורא then given birth through the Name אלהים/**Elohim**, Mother to Creation constantly murmuring in each vibration and color blanketing the Earth תבל, so בורא can be known in low.

Paragraph Seven

כד אתתקן לבתר נקודה והיכלא כחדא, כדין, בראשית כליל ראשיתא עלאה בחכמתא. לבתר אתחלף גוון ההוא היכלא ואקרי בית נקודה עלאה אקרי ראש. כליל דא ברזא בראשית, כד איהו כלא כחדא בכללא חדא עד לא הוי ישובא בביתא, כיון אזדרע לתקונא דישובא, כדין אקרי אלהים טמירא סתימא.

אתתקן לבתר נקודה והיכלא כחדא כדין בראשית כליל ראשיתא עלאה בחכמתא

Construction In Place of the Dot and Chamber As One Ordered בראשית/In the Beginning Includes Beginning Above With Chochma/Logic

The construction of the universe begins in earnest after the BlackWhole. No instrument can pierce the fierceness of light and energy emanating from the point tethering the stars of our galaxy, including our solar system. But in the beginning of creation, as the shards of light streamed out of the engraving from the Name אלהים/**Elohim** while yet connected to the source, was commanded through the Name י-ה-ו-ה. Therefore, though light is divided into threads of luminescence, they are essentially unified. Yet, the Oneness of the Creator is not of creation, in any way or manner.

The six letters in the first word in the Torah בראשית/**In the Beginning** incorporates the word ראש/**Head**. The Word ישראל/**Yisroel-Israel** can be rearranged to read ראש לי/**Rosh Li-My Head**. The Head is the beginning of logic. Beyond logic is Will and Pleasure, the crowning components of existence keeping us invigorated. The word חכמה/**Chochma-Wisdom** refers to the right side of the brain where the soul enters into the body keeping the brain in a state of constant thought from the feet of the soul running inside the head of the person.

The word חכמה/**Wisdom** can be broken down into חכ מה/**Power of What** the power to ask a question from what is seen. The left side of the brain is feminine, the bastion of hearing. תורה/**Torah** means **Teaching**; the teacher wants the students to ask questions—revealing the recognition of logic. There is no dogma in the words of תורה. From the beginning of creation, logic rules. When scientists find an anomaly in nature, the entire scholastic world trembles. Creation began with a desire, which is a reflection of hidden pleasure, far beyond logic. The wisdom of חכמה through the vehicle of the question begins the pathway to logic.

לבתר אתחלף גוון ההוא היכלא ואקרי בית נקודה עלאה אקרי ראש.

In the Place Exchanging Colors In The Chamber Called House of Supernal Dot Called Rosh/Head

The introduction of color indicates sine waves of various vibrations interacting in the prism of creation where ephemeral structures are created then destroyed like a painter painting a picture layer upon layer until satisfaction is achieved. The right side of the brain corresponding to the eyes is colored silver; the left side of the brain corresponding to the ears is colored gold—the third eye corresponding to the two nostrils colored copper. Color is the first vibration from נקדה/**Dot** known as the BlackWhole along with the sound אמש/**Emesh** bringing about the three higher elements: fire, air and water on a mission from בורא to be known in low.

Once put into motion, the universe continues in a way of cause and effect based on logic. As is said, God made Creation בחכמה/**With Wisdom**. The נקדה/**Dot** of creation, known as the Black-Whole is the ראש/**Rosh-Head**. Independence begins from the head. When the head of the child enters into the world, independence is achieved. The beginning of the Hebrew year is ראש השנה/**Rosh HaShana-Head of the Year**. The heavenly decree for the coming yearly cycle is written into the **Head of the Year** during the two days of ראש השנה/**Rosh HaShana-Head of The Year** corresponding the two hemispheres of the brain, dispersing life into the body through time.

Ten days after hearing the שופר/**Shofar-Ram's Horn** being sounded on ראש השנה/**Rosh HaShana-Head of The Year** concludes the process. The third aspect to the head is accomplished tens days later by fasting on **Yom Kippur/Day of Atonement** corresponding to the third eye, depicted by the two nostrils. The right and the left hemispheres of the brain think in a way of hearing and seeing but the third eye suddenly just knows, as a result of cognition. The function of knowing is to momentarily shut down the apparatus of thought, allowing cognition to come to a conclusion, knowing.

Thinking is the most spiritual bodily activity. The brain is able to imagine anything and everything with the exception of בורא who is unimaginable, being neither of שמים/**Shamayim-Heaven** or ארץ/**Eretz-Earth**. Also, thoughts have no weight, as in Heaven where the heaviness of corporality does not exist. Sex is the lowest activity of the body. Our galaxy begins in the head then comes down to the Earth called תבל with a gematria of 432—the resonance of the ground measured in hertz. The word תבל refers to a human being and an animal having sex. Each person is comprised of an animal soul and a human soul living together in one body on planet Earth.

כליל דא ברזא בראשית כד איהו כלא כחדא בכללא חדא עד
לא הוי ישובא בביתא כיון אזדרע לתקונא דישובא כדין אקרי
אלהים טמירא סתימא.

Included In the Secret Beginning Until All is One Awaiting Return Home Since Seeding Accomplishes Return Order is Called Hidden אלהים

All of the knowledge concerning creation is hinted at in the word בראשית/**In the Beginning**. Similar to how the functions of the body trace back to the brain. Creation is constructed by the design of בורא inside the BlackWhole conducting the galaxy of stars. The Dot is called ראשית/**Beginning** the head of the galaxy where all knowledge is stored and revealed at the proper time. זהר is a knowledge from beyond the far side of the BlackWhole into the primordial chamber from where creation is continually conceived. Yet, everything was considered static since return had yet to happen.

When בורא said די/**Di-Enough** to the static expansion, reality ballooned instantly expanding then suddenly halting causing refraction to happen as creation slowed down to the speed of light. The dispersed light is equated with throwing seeds into the fallow soil. The seed causes the ground to grow in much the way the seed of man causes the woman to be impregnated but the woman grows the baby not the sperm. Each beam of light between the spectrum from blue to red is a seed planted in the abyss, sprouting worlds without end and life without measure. From the universe down, all of creation is created from עיץ חיים/**Tree of Life.**

A similar pattern is followed in the Name אלהים/**Elohim**; חסד/**Kindness** is hidden through the attribute of the final two letters making the word ים/**Ocean**—the word אלהים has a gematria of 86 the same הטבע/**HaTeva-The Nature** related to the word הטבע/**Hatbaya-Sunken**. When light pierces water, the shaft of light appears altered, a protection for fish but also a sign: Mother

Nature is a shield against the light י-ה-ו-ה by אלהים. Only when the Creator בורא is hidden from creation can freedom of choice exist. In Heaven, there is light but there is no freedom of choice.

Paragraph Eight

זהר סתים וגנין עד דבנין בגויה לאלדא, וביתא קיימא בפשיטו דאינון זרע קדש. זהרועד לא אתעדיאת, ולא אתפשט פשיטו דישובאת לא אקרי אלהים, אלא כלא בכללא בראשית, לבתר דאתתקן בשמא דאלהים, אפיק אינון תולדין מההוא זרעא דאזדרע ביה. מאן ההוא זרעא אינון אתוון גליפן רזא דאורייתא דנפקו מההיא נקודה.

זהר סתים וגנין עד דבנין בגויה לאלדא וביתא קיימא בפשיטו דאינון זרע קדש

זהר Hides And Protects until the Construction Within Bears Fruit Establishing a House by Expressing These Separated Seeds

The inside of the BlackWhole hides and protects the Chamber of Conception revealed in the construction within the abyss עץ חיים/**Tree of Life** continues to bear fruit trying to achieve God's Desire to be known in low. The confines of creation are defined by the expression of the stars tracing back to the original spark, shards from the primordial engraving into the crown of the BlackWhole producing seeds separated from the עץ חיים.

The Preface to the זהר begins by describing creation as a rose amid thorns. The Name אלהים/**Elohim** is the flower to creation dispersing seeds in the form of stars, shards from the original engraving. Compared to the Flower of God depicted by the עץ חיים/**Tree of Life** the stars are but thorns pricking the expanse of space. The word קדש means, Separate. These shards we call stars are remnants from the Oneness existing at the far side of the BlackWhole from where the knowledge of זהר is founded. The Talmud depicts Creation as a loom threaded with light.

Just as creation came from Oneness, so too Oneness is forever implicit within creation, a web of light pulling and pushing at astronomical levels. Our universe is God's House of Light. At first, we only saw the stars, then scientists introduced us to the galaxy, then many galaxies until the entire expanse of the universe, though bounded by time and space, is full of the unimaginable. Crushing puny scientific theories beneath the vast weight of implicit form; creation is the masterpiece from בורא—massive galaxies threaded together with other massive galaxies until the universe is one, a beautiful diamond spinning within the darkness of infinity.

ועד לא אתעדיאת ולא אתפשט פשיטו דישובאת לא אקרי
אלהים אלא כלא בכללא בראשית

Until Time Began No Expression in Return Name Elohim Not Called All included in בראשית/In the Beginning

Time is a function of movement shackled to a constant, the speed of light. Prior to the speed of light, creation was unencumbered by confines. Everything happened instantaneously while time was unable to catch up; space was like a gapping mouth—until there is return, there is no movement and no time. From the BlackWhole until the advent of stars is considered the Two Thousand Years בורא played with creation before creating the Six Days of Creation 266,450,000 years later. Time could not begin until return was introduced. God Said, go out and create, but בורא Said nothing about returning or being separated, that job was left to the human being.

אור/**Light** like fire is endemically high since the nature of fire and light is to go up, constantly striving to become closer to the source of fire. But, בורא wanted to be known in low, so בורא made a separation between the source of light and the little packets of light strewn throughout space. A line of light is forever connected to the source, any interruption is like a cloud before the sun. So בורא made creation stop, causing the reverberation to slow down to the speed of light.

In the קבלה/**Cabala**, these three stages are called: עקודים/**Aku-dim-Lines**; נקודים/ **Nekudim-Dots**; ברודים/**Brudim-Separation**: Line -Dot-Separation.

לבתר דאתתקן בשמא דאלהים אפיק אינון תולדין מההוא
זרעא דאזדרע ביה מאן ההוא זרעא אינון אתוון גליפן רזא
דאורייתא דנפקו מההיא נקודה

In this Place Established Name Elohim Going Out is Birthed the Seed Seeded Within From That Seed Signs of Engraving Hinting to Truth Going Out From the Dot

Everything in creation is an expression from אלהים/**Elohim**, residing in the ראשית/**Beginning** of creation from the BlackWhole in the center of our galaxy. The Name אלהים is Mother to creation; from her comes all the souls—the angels and entities are more diverse than the creatures of the sea. Whatever exists, traces back to the Name אלהים cloaked in Nature. Yet, with each breaking, negativity is released creating an obstruction, frustration on a galactic scale is manifested. Each shard is a Name of בורא, as **Dovid** המלך/**HaMelch-The King** sings, God counts by Name all the stars each night.

Once the Name אלהים/**Elohim** is carved into the כתר/**Crown** upon the aperture leading to the universe on one side and to the inner sanctum on the other side, then the separated seeds of creation expanded until commanded to stop, causing the universe to refract as if light were trying to penetrate an ocean of water. Each spark from the engraving becomes a letter until the entire story of the universe is written into a book illuminated in the heavens. Now the time has come to write the conclusion to these last six thousand years of male dominance upon תבל/**Earth**, the lowest most physical place in the creation.

An attribute of שמים/**Heaven** is life exists within but here on תבל life exists on the exterior of the planet. We cover death with the ground. All life seeded throughout the universe and all the reverberations and declinations throughout creation are focused on תבל because here is where the Desire of בורא can finally be fulfilled. Each spark in the universe is a letter chipped from the Name of בורא; each soul is engraved from within a star—every aspect of creation is pinned to תבל.

The seeds given off by the Supernal Rose, letters chipped from the Name of בורא is a hint to the תורה which was similarly chipped from a cube of sapphire, engraving the Ten Commandments. Each shard from the original engraving was a letter inscribed by the Finger of God. There are 600,000 letters and spaces by which בורא and the Prophet משה/Moshe constructed the תורה the first five books. The process of engraving is how the light and the knowledge is transmitted from the other side of the BlackWhole where God's Desire to be known in low is twisted into light.

Paragraph Nine

ההיא נקודה זרע בגו ההוא היכלא רזא דתלת נקודין: חלם שורק, חירק, ואתכלילו דא בדא, קול דנפיק בחבורא חדא. בשעתא דנפק, נפקת בת זוגיה בהדיה, דכליל כל אתוון דכתיב את השמים, קול ובת זוגו. האי קול דאיהו שמים. איהו אהיה בתראה. זהר דכליל כל אתוון וגוונין כגוונא דא.

ההיא נקודה זרע בגו ההוא היכלא רזא דתלת נקודין: חלם שורק חירק ואתכלילו דא בדא קול דנפיק בחבורא חדא.
This Dot of Seed within the Chamber Hints At Three Dots: חלם שורק חירק (three vocalizations indicated by a dot above, a dot in the middle and a dot below a letter.) **Infused One With the Other until a Voice Goes Out In Inclusion**

The individual seed while within the inner chamber is infused with three points in the triangulated form of the letter י/Yud. The letter י/Yud no more than a dot, the smallest of the 22 Hebrew letters, is employed at the head of the engraving tool produced by God's Desire, but even this sharp point is made from three points, as pictured in the letter **י/Yud**. The letter **י/Yud** is comprised of a tiny horn on top of the dot and a little horn at the bottom of the dot, as if to say, energy went in and energy went out leaving a dot in the middle hinting at past, present and future.

The vocalizations of the letters are part of the Oral Tradition but in modern books these points of sound are printed along with the letter, helping the reader to pronounce the word correctly. In תורה the pronunciation is not as important as the clarity of the written word. **חלם/Choolum** is an **O** sound inscribed as a dot on top of the letter; **שורק/Shorook** the **OO** sound is marked by a dot at the middle of a letter and **חירק/Chirik** an **E** sound is a dot at the bottom of the letter." O-OO-E. Each hand-written letter in the Torah begins with a **י/Yud-Dot** then with a fine feathered pen, the scribe draws each letter out from within the dot of ink.

Thus, top, middle and bottom are established along with the primordial pool of letters as conceived in the Inner Chamber inside the BlackWhole. Sight and sound became one as a voice was emitted in the form of the letters **אמש/Emesh** establishing the three upper elements: **אש/Aish-fire**; **אוויר/Avir-air** and **מים/Mayim-water**. Our constantly vibrating universe is singing to בורא. Everywhere throughout creation, the Creator is recognized, even on planet תבל with the exception of the human being who questions the existence of בורא. Each human being is the lowest place in creation, possessing free will to chose a path in life according to the perception of our circumstance.

בשעתא דנפק, נפקת בת זוגיה בהדיה, דכליל כל אתוון דכתיב
את השמים, קול ובת זוגו

When Going Out Went Out Mate Together Includes All Letters As Written את השמים/The Heaven

The going out from the resultant shards of engraving Name **אלהים/Elohim** in the outer rim of the BlackWhole included a clear function of reception. Meaning, the dualistic nature of creation combines both male and female aspects of in and out. Creation in the beginning was clearly androgynous. A way of attenuating the light by chipping away at אמת/**Truth** scattered shards everywhere yet coalescing all the light into one place, the word תבל describes the collusion of male and female, human and animal energy within each person. The word תבל has a gematria of 432, the resonance of the global vibration at 432 hertz.

The beginning of תורה starts with בורא Creating את השמים/**The Heaven.** The word שמים/**Heaven** is a combination of אש/**Fire** and מים/**Water** but the term את has no meaning whatsoever. זוהר explains in שיר השירים/**Song of Songs** how the two extremities of the 22 letters את (א is the first letter who is male and ת is the last letter who is female) while the other twenty letters are a combination of male and female. By putting together the א/**Aleph** and ת/**Tof** God is able to experience male and female combined, giving birth to the heavens. Similarly בורא created את הארץ/**The Earth.** בורא is neither spiritual nor physical. בורא is אחד/**Echud-One**, Creator of both the physical and the spiritual.

Light and sound operate on vibration, one faster and one slower, replicated in sight which can see a long distance and sound which is conveyed in closer quarters. Every experience is interwoven with ambient sight and sound. There is a beautiful song vibrating throughout the universe but those of us who inhabit the Earth are deaf; there is beautiful form to creation but those of us who inhabit the Earth are blind—history follows the spiral of time constantly coming to conclusion. Illumination is coming to the world; those awake need to waken others—as the brilliance of זהר meant for our time is arousing the sleeping to blink away ignorance.

האי קול דאיהו שמים. איהו אהיה בתראה. זהר דכליל כל אתוון וגוונין כגוונא דא

The Voice is Heaven. The Last Iteration of the Future. Zohar Combines All Letters and Colors

The tenth and final component comprising the עיץ חיים/Tree of Life is called מלכות/Malchut-Royalty because the king rules from verbal decree through the spoken word of the king. The BlackWhole is continually mouthing creation into being, murmuring in bountiful beautiful adulations a song of life for all who live. Life is everywhere, even vacuous space is alive with meaning because nothing escapes the watchful of Eye of בורא who loves creation and wants only to be acknowledged as the provider to all. Asking of the human being only to obey the Seven Commandments, first of which is not to pray to the heavens, because God is everywhere. What does בורא want? God wants a relationship on low.

Between the BlackWhole and the human being is the conduit called שמים transferring articulations in the same way human beings speak to a very young child. Only בורא and the human being have the capacity to articulate thoughts into words because all of creation exists only as an intermediary, as expressed in the equation: 365 squared times two thousand equaling 266,450,000 broken down into the secret timing of creation when 26/God through the Six Days of Creation, prototype to the six thousand years of male agenda connects with **45/Human Being.**

בורא is having a relationship with every human being on Earth during these six thousand years, so בורא can be known in low. Each person on Earth, for a brief span of time, has the opportunity to know בורא in whatever way deemed real and honest within the confines of the Seven Commandments given to all peoples of the world. When we the people of the world finally open our collective eyes, we will see the beautiful paradise made by our Creator בורא from a pebble beneath the Throne of God. This pebble will forever give life. She is our Mother Earth constantly percolating with life. When the false veneer and the stench of religion is wiped from the globe and the gleam of silver no longer blinds the eye, then reality will become obvious.

Paragraph Ten

עד הכא י-ה-ו-ה אלהינו י-ה-ו-ה אלין תלתא דרגין לקבל רזא דא עלאה בראשית ברא אלהים בראשית רזא קדמאה ברא רזא סתימא לאתפשטא מתמן כלא אלהים רזא לקיימא כלא לתתא. את השמים דלא לאפרשא לון דכר ונוקבא כחדא.

עד הכא י-ה-ו-ה אלהינו י-ה-ו-ה אלין תלתא דרגין לקבל רזא דא עלאה בראשית ברא אלהים בראשית רזא קדמאה ברא רזא סתימא לאתפשטא מתמן כלא אלהים רזא לקיימא כלא לתתא **יהוה אלהינו יהוה Until Now These Three Levels To Receive Supernal Secret בראשית ברא אלהים/In The Beginning God Created. בראשית/In The Beginning Hints at Beginning. ברא/Created Hints Secret Ejaculating From There All Is אלהים/Elohim Secret to Establishing Everything Below**

The Name י-ה-ו-ה is comprised of four letters which when rearranged render the three different aspects of time: היה/**Past**; הוה/**Present**; יהיה/**Future** indicating time prior to the creation of time. Through the intercession from the Name אלהים/**Elohim**, the י-ה-ו-ה is replicated into the עיץ חיים portrayed in the symmetry of the solar system, geography of the Earth the form of the human being built on three triangles plus the power of speech. Symmetry and order is an explicit expression of logic; cause and effect brings cognition into chaos where the genesis to creation is formed—all creation is made to fulfill God's Desire to be known in low.

The origin of order comes from the juxtaposition of Names, beginning with the Name י-ה-ו-ה on a level beyond time and space filtered through the Name אלהים/**Elohim** turning the Oneness into multiplicity before returning back into י-ה-ו-ה in the form of the solar system, the geography of the Earth תבל and the symmetry implicit in every human form. Similarly, light slows when going through a pane of glass then resumes the speed of light on the other side of the glass. This natural phenomenon is emblematic of the creation process where the Light of בורא is the same on both sides of creation.

The correlations and consistencies seen throughout creation corroborates the intricacies with which the universe is made; from the starlight woven together as a bed upon which י-ה-ו-ה the male attribute of God is interwoven with the Name אלהים/Elohim, the female attribute of God—Mother and Father to Creation. The Love shared between these two Names is the source of all love. The experience of love incessantly evokes the Name of God from the two lovers because love brings us to the fountainhead of creation, בראשית ברא אלהים/In The Beginning God Created.

These first three words in the Torah correspond to: ה-ו-י ה-ו-ה-י אלהינו. Truly, **In the Beginning** brought forth י-ה-ו-ה who brought forth אלהים/Elohim who then created creation in the form of the י-ה-ו-ה. The תורה is meant to be read on four levels with each word having seventy windows into different paths of interpretation without contradiction to any other path. The Rabbis who wrote down the Oral Law two thousand years ago were called חברים/**Chavirim-Friends** because, though they argued, they never contradicted; they sharpened their minds against the steel of their friend—the words of the תורה on all four levels are etched into the heart of each Jewish soul.

את השמים דלא לאפרשא לון דכר ונוקבא כחדא
את השמים/The Heavens Not Separated, Male And female Like One

The word את/Et has no literal meaning, yet את corresponds to the two aspects of male and female portrayed in the first and last letters of the 22 letter Hebrew alphabet. By establishing gender within the words of the תורה allows בורא to interface with creation according to established laws of nature emanating from the collusion between י-ה-ו-ה and אלהים. The phrase את השמים/**The Heavens** indicates how Heaven is made from male and female aspects. The process of creation from the את is likened to how children are conceived here on our terrestrial planet. The collusion between two, producing a third.

The beginning of creation was androgynous from the very onset, as male and female created creation together without separation. The anomaly of physical light moving at the speed of light, which is the constant to the universe displaying a ray with the properties of matter bending around the Moon during an eclipse, rendering a weaving together of the Names incorporated in the process, a continual continuity of creation. Creation is played out upon the Earth as the human being dances the dance of life with love in their heart because God is being known in low.

The word **זכר/Zaakor-Male** means Remember in Hebrew; while **נשים/Noshim-Female** in Hebrew means, **Forget** in Aramaic. The way of man is to remember, seeking justice; while woman tends to forget and just go on having compassion—creation pulses between these two opposites. Woman is likened to a circle and man to a line, when the two unite a spiral emerges. Blessings from בורא only comes when male and female are interwoven together. There are many expressions of male and female throughout creation. How we chose to honor this intrinsic relationship is reflected in our respect for creation and Creator everywhere in all expressions.

Paragraph Eleven

את כד נטיל אתוון כלהון כללא דכלהו אתוון אינון רישא וסיפא. לבתר אתוסף ה"א, לאתחברא כלהו אתוון בה"א, ואתקרי אתה. ועל דא ואת"ה מחיה את כלם. א"ת, רזא אדני והכי אקרי. השמים דא יהו רזא עלאה.

את כד נטיל אתוון כלהון כללא דכלהו אתוון אינון רישא וסיפא. לבתר אתוסף ה"א לאתחברא כלהו אתוון בה"א ואתקרי אתה
את Includes All Letters All letters Have a Head and an End. After Adding ה/Hey Combines All Letters With ה/Hey Producing אתה/You

The letter ה/**Hey-5** is the least articulated sound from the 22 letters, requiring merely an expiration of breath to accomplish the pronunciation of the letter ה/**Hey-5**. To the Creator, all of creation is merely an exhalation of breath requiring minimal effort. The word את combined with the letter ה makes the word: אתה/**You**. Awakening to God results from the recognition of בורא within the workings and confines of creation. The initial cognition of other is contained in the word אתה/**You**. The word אתה/**You** contains all the letters making up creation based on the ten attributes from the עיץ חיים plus the Breath of בורא blown into life, the letter ה.

The עיץ חיים is portrayed in our solar system as the Sun and the nine planets. The last planet, Pluto corresponds with the final attribute known as מלכות/**Royalty** equated with speech. Speech has five aspects: throat, pallet, tongue, teeth and lips and the planet Pluto has five moons. The two planets between the Sun and the Earth, Venus and Mercury, have no moons and no life. The Sun, Mercury and Venus correspond to the three parts of the brain: right hemisphere, left hemisphere and third eye. From תבל on out, there is life in plentitude with moons and asteroids all feeding תבל with needed nutrients from space.

These outer six planets make up what is known as the Seven רקיעים/**Heavens** where spiritual life teems with greater diversity than what is found beneath the surface of the sea. By seeing the innate structure behind creation reflecting the עיץ חיים/**Tree of Life** a person is forced to confront בורא. In all Jewish prayers בורא is called by the term אתה/**You**. In translating the תורה many translators try to give elevation to the words by using flowery language, when the opposite is true. אתה/**You** is the most common way to speak which is what בורא wants from creation. Just be real, be humble before the Creator of Heaven and Earth.

ועל דא ואת"ה מחיה את כלם. א"ת, רזא אדני והכי אקרי.
השמים דא יהו רזא עלאה

On This word את"ה/You All Is Enlivened. א"ת Is Called Secret אדני/Master. Heaven is יהו Supernal Secret

From the word את everything is created but from the word אתה/**You** everything is enliven. There is no noun or pronoun able to describe בורא but the word אתה shows a recognition of בורא who wants to be known in low. The recognition of בורא through the intercession of the word אתה is the beginning of that process. In every revelation is found the humility of God being lowered into this world known as אתה. But, this is what בורא wants from creation. Lofty words are lost on God.

There are seven Names of בורא written in the Torah which are not allowed to be erased. They are: יה/**Ya**, אל/**El**, אלהים/**Elohim**, שדי/**Shaddai**, י-ה-ו-ה/**Y-H-V-H**, צבאת/**Tzevaot**, אדני/**Adonai**. The last of the Seven Names, אדני/**Master** is interposed with the four letters from י-ה-ו-ה which rules during the day while אדני rules at night. The Name י-ה-ו-ה is impossible to pronounce so the Name אדני is used instead. Not only is בורא beyond creation but so too is the pronunciation and translation י-ה-ו-ה is beyond word. Only through the intercession of the Name אדני/**Master** and **Royalty** can the intense light from the Creator enter into the world.

א״ת תקונא דכר ונוקבא. וא״ת רזא הויה, וכלא חד

את Establishes Male and Female And את Hints to י-ה-ו-ה All is One

In all Jewish prayers, בורא is referred to as מלך העולם/**Meleck Ha-Olam-King of the World**. Even though each person is בני/**Child** to בורא we are all also subject to the Royal Command, the Seven Commandments to the people of the world and the 613 Commandments to the Jewish People, for which we were chosen—The Chosen People. The heavens are composed from the first three letters from the י-ה-ו-ה. The first three letters יהו are the source to the three elements which make up Heaven: fire, air and water. Thus the name for Heaven is שא מים/**Sa Mayim-Hold Water**. The final ה, the Breath of God, is the source to the Earth תבל.

Paragraph Twelve

א"ת, תקונא דכר ונוקבא. וא"ת, רזא הויה, וכלא חד. את הארץ דא אלהים, כגוונא עלאה למעבד פירין ואיבין. שמא דא כלילא בתלת דוכתי, ומתמן אתפרש שמא דא לכמה סטרין. עד הכא רזא דסתרא דסתרין, דגליף ובני, וקיים בארח סתים בסתרא דחד קרא.

א"ת, תקונא דכר ונוקבא. וא"ת, רזא הויה, וכלא חד

The א"ת is the completion of male and female. א"ת is the secret to the י-ה-ו-ה and everything is One

Life is confined between male and female plus all the infinite mixtures and blends found throughout creation. The Hebrew language is written in these two genders using the twenty letters situated between the first letter א' the male paradigm and the last letter ת the female paradigm. Male and female are equally depicted in the formation of the י-ה-ו-ה. A stick figure of a human being emerges when the four letters are set vertically as does the human skeleton when lying supine in the grave. The Name pervades all, rendering the entirety as One. The concept of One shows on God's ability to be everywhere all the time to every aspect of creation, undeterred by duality.

Male energy goes out while female energy goes in, causing male and female to be as two different species, two threads in the loom of life going in opposite directions. The source of male and female is found in the Name י-ה-ו-ה. The letters י and ה are also referred to as Father and Mother. The ו and ה is considered male and female. The Name י-ה-ו-ה threads throughout creation uniting each atom of creation into a whole. The other side of the BlackWhole is the י' from the Name י-ה-ו-ה known by the cabalists as אצילות/**Atzilut-Close**.

The BlackWhole constitutes the beginning of creation, depicted by the first ה/**Hey** from the Name י-ה-ו-ה known as בריה/**Creation** from where the universe is birthed. The letter ו/**Vav** corresponds to the universe divided into twelve segments depicted in zodical images called יצירה/**Form** known as the Twelve Diagonals . The final letter ה/**Hey** corresponds to our solar system and is called by the term

עשיה/**Action**. In this way, all of creation is One through the apparatus of the Four Letter Name י-ה-ו-ה. The Earth is **עשיה גשמי/Asiyia Goshmia-Physical Action**, the only place in creation where free choice exists and commandments can be done.

> הארץ דא אלהים כגוונא עלאה למעבד פירין ואיבין שמא דא
> כלילא בתלת דוכתי ומתמן אתפרש שמא דא לכמה סטרין
> **The Earth אלהים Designed from High to Produce Fruits And Plants. This Name Includes Three Dimensions And From There, Spreads This Name To Many Directions**

The duality of creation divides between the highest point in Heaven and the lowest point on Earth. The original engraving of the Name **אלהים/Elohim** onto the lips of the BlackWhole culminates upon the Earth with a universe in between. The voice of every person on Earth is transmitted through the planets to the five moons of Pluto from where articulation into celestial speech filters through a universe of stars, kissed by angels on their way to the center of our galaxy. From the Name אלהים the Name associated with plurality, is hidden the secret of birth and the bearing of fruits.

The Name אלהים is a combination of kindness and severity merged together through the letter 'ה associated with the five severities corresponding to the five moons around Pluto. Whereas the four letters of י-ה-ו-ה comprise Oneness, the five letters of אלהים comprise a continually expanding plurality due to the contraction of birth. The seed of birth is delivered by man but after the seed rots, the process happens through woman. Strength is commiserate with contraction; engaging muscles requires contraction—the opposite of contraction are the waters of kindness. Contraction breaks apart while water brings together. The seed must first decay before the ground can grow.

The three divisions of the Name אלהים produce the three dimensions of space: height, width and breath filled with nature growing like a pregnant woman until manifesting upon the Earth in a physical dimension surrounded by a spiritual universe feeding all the components of life through the web of universal light. This process took 266,450,000 years before the stars clicked on, this number is approximately confirmed by science. Just as the seed from the father exists within the fruit of the womb, so too does י-ה-ו-ה pervade creation implicit within the Name אלהים.

עד הכא רזא דסתרא דסתרין דגליף ובני וקיים בארח סתים
בסתרא דחד קרא

Until Now Hinted from Hidden of Hiding, The Engraving and Shards Existing Hidden Expanse In One

The תורה can be read on four levels with each word having seventy faces, all laced together into one reality whose only aim is to satisfy the Desire of בורא to be known in low. The meticulous details hidden in זהר was saved for our time when technology allows the secrets of the universe to be probed. Ancient people had no need for technology since they clearly saw the symmetry of creation עיץ חיים/**Tree of Life**. And, although all people struggle to understanding the genesis of existence, no one thought until our time that creation just happened, like a big bang. Ridiculous.

בורא wants to be acknowledged throughout the world as being מלך העולם/**King of the World** corresponding to the final letter ה/**Hey** in the י-ה-ו-ה related to speech through the attribution of the King verbally enacting decrees. God spoke and the world was. Only בורא and the human being speak, while the rest of creation can only utter emotional sounds. The gematria of י-ה-ו-ה is 26. We are 26 thousand lightyears from the center of our galaxy and we appear to be revolving around the North Star every 26,000 years and the world pulses every 26 seconds. Seeing the symmetry of creation, is to acknowledge בורא within each animated aspect of life. The First Commandment of the 613 Commandments given to the Jewish People is to know God, later we are commanded to love God yet neither knowing nor love can be commanded, instead they must come of their own volition. Knowing is a function of experience, when the infant touches the fire through the experience of pain, the child now knows fire is hot, burning hot. To know בורא we must experience life with God, a trusted companion through the darkness of this physical world.

Paragraph Thirteen

מכאן והלאה בראשית ברא שית, מקצה השמים ועד קצה השמים שית סטרין דמתפשטן מרזא עלאה באתפשטותא דברא, מגו נקידה קדמאה ברא אתפשטותא דחד נקודה דלעילא והכא אגליף רזא שמא דארבעין ותרין אתוון.

מכאן והלאה בראשית ברא שית מקצה השמים ועד קצה השמים שית סטרין דמתפשטן מרזא עלאה באתפשטותא דברא
From Here and Further בראשית is ברא/Created שית/Six From The Edges Of Heaven Until Six Sides Of Proliferation Hinting From Above In Diversification Of Creation

The initial chaos at the very beginning of creation when the shards from the engraving of the Name אלהים/**Elohim** upon the lips of the BlackWhole was the beginning of separation and individuality. Each separate shard was suddenly not part of the whole, harbinger to the first existential thought, Who am I? Where am I going? People often feel alienated at times when suddenly divorced or lose a job, a feeling tracing back to this primordial disconnection. בורא is said to have played with creation for two thousand years prior to creation—365 squared times 2000 equals 266,450,000 a code: **26/God; 6/Six Days of Creation** culminating with **45/Adom-Man** beginning the six thousand years of man.

Outside the bubble of our solar system is a realm unlike anything anywhere, this is where the stars are set into the ebony atmosphere seeded with BlackWholes within the all encompassing first contraction called חוקם פני/**Mokim Ponai-Empty Space** causing the first expansion of space. But, beyond what is seen and measured are massive clumps of darkness with a pull but no substance. These chambers, called Dark Matter by scientists are the place for angels where spiritual happenings take place within chambers each with a שער/**Shar-Gate** whose letters can be reverse to read עשר/**Eser-Ten**—עיץ חיים/ **Tree of Life**.

In the space of creation, is established the six dimensions within a confine able to be attenuated down until the original intention of Creator twisted into the **OreAinSof/LightWithoutEnd** can be realized in our tiny solar system of ten, on the outskirts of a galaxy amid a myriad profusion of galaxies and wonders spread throughout the universe. When the expansion of creation halted at the Creator's Shout די/**Di-Enough** the stars blinked on with light tethered immediately to our place in the universe where God's Desire is being fulfilled. The beginning of creation is found in the word בראשית/**In the Beginning** rearranged to write ברא שית/**Bara Shesh-Created Six**.

מגו נקידה קדמאה ברא אתפשטותא דחד נקודה דלעילא
והכא אגליף רזא שמא דארבעין ותרין אתוון

Coming from Within the Primordial Dot Created Expansion From One Supernal Dot Above From Where Engraved Secret Name with 42 Letters

The word אחד/**Echud-One** can be interpreted by separating each letter implying: א/**Aleph-One** inside the ח/**Chet-Eight**, Seven Heavens and the Earth plus the ד/**Daled-Four** directions upon תבל. These declinations of three letters expresses how בורא is One within the dualistic creation of multiplicity, buffered by the universe. The Creator is able to be known through the Seven Heavens divided by the six outer planets to the Earth where each person stands on the top of the globe with four direction to express free choice: North, East, South and West. The human being is considered מהלך/**MaHaluch-Walker**. ארץ/**Eretz-Earth** can be reduced down to רץ א'/**I Run**.

There are many Names within the BlackWhole but the Name מב/**Mob-42** the number comprising the concept of confusion called תהו/**Tohu-Chaos** is the final primal genesis of creation. The number 42 pertains to chaos because six times seven equals 42, meaning chaos is missing a seven which is established on תבל where seven continents support terrestrial life. The planet Mars is the final iteration of תהו/**Tohu-Chaos**. On תהו/**Tohu-Chaos** the seeds of creation were gathered from the stars down through the planets until in the cavernous innards of the planet Mars, the ancients referred to ציא/**Ztia-Dry**, until a burst oceanic water from deep within the belly of Mars caused a stream of water connecting to תבל delivering life in the form of seeds.

The Earth is known to be the place of תיקון/**Tikun-Fixing** by drawing the chaos into order. In the previous world of תהו/**Tohu-Chaos** through 974 generations on Mars the culmination of universal contraction bringing seeds of life to Earth was forged along with woman. Without man, sex was dormant. Woman wanting sex precipitated man created upon the Earth with woman within. Earth and Mars are both woman, one fire within with a calm multi-colored exterior while the other is the opposite, calm within with a harsh red exterior.

These two woman are depicted in Chava and Lilith, the first two women along with the first man. Lilith came as a result of creation; Chava came from a pebble beneath the Throne of the Creator—together these two primordial woman gave birth to man, who needs refinement to merge with woman in 220 years at the advent of the Thousand Years of Woman and Peace.

These first 13 paragraphs in the Book זהר are an independent section setoff from what follows. The number 13 is the gematria אחד/**Echud-One**. The highest point in prayer is pronouncing the word אחד. To extend that pronunciation is to extend one's life.

Chapter Eight

WHY 2020

זהר was written in Heaven a thousand years after Rebbe Shimmon passed away from memories he took with him to Heaven. The amazing conversations concerning תורה during his time on Earth two thousand years ago were possessed in Heaven as a concordance of material by which to cloth the brilliant light from the other side of the BlackWhole. Rebbe Shimmon was able to sneak the knowledge of זהר down to תבל by disguising the Truth in Aramaic, a language unknown to the angels who guard שער השמים/**Gates of Heaven**. Also, as part of the needed attenuation from שמים to תבל, the Book זהר reads easier in Aramaic than the original Hebrew etched into the firmament of Heaven. This sublime knowledge was immediately recognized by those enmeshed in תורה yet none could untangle the mystery incapsulated in these words. Even now, those with a clear understanding of ancient Hebrew and Aramaic are dumbfounded by the concepts proposed in the text plus descriptions of worlds unknown to the Earth. Yet, scattered throughout are amazing insights into אמת/**Truth** which only someone of Rebbe Shimmon's stature could have delivered.

Towards the end of the massively worded text of זהר Rebbe Shimmon exclaims, These words are meant for the סוף ימים/**End of Days** without giving an explanation as to why? There are many visions and prophesies concerning these End Times throughout תורה many prophesies manifest in every generation, but our time is different because of 777. The 777 is the gematria of God's futuristic Name אהיה/**Ehiye-Future**. Seven concludes the Six Days of Creation with the Seventh Day of Rest. Seven indicates end. What the

Jewish People know as the Two Thousand Year Exile of Rome is ending. Now is when זהר is needed and can be understood.

The six thousand year Hebrew calendar, like the five thousand year Mayan calendar, has a precise beginning and end. The Roman calendar is capricious, a mythical beginning continuing without an end. Rome's conquest of the world has solidified in America where in the year 2017/5777 an eclipse of the Sun by the Moon crossed the Bible Belt of America; in the same year, Trump was elected president—the beginning of the end. When Trump was inaugurated he was seventy years, seven months and seven days. By 2020, fifty years since the human specie reached the half-life of carbon-14, the World Health Organization declared Covid-19 a pandemic on March 11, 2020 when there were seven billion seven hundred million and seventy million people on the Earth, תבל —7,770,000.

The end is apparent. The end of the male agenda which has charted a drunken path off to oblivion fueled by the lie. זהר clearly establishes the confines of creation and how God's Will is being played out on תבל as if a play of six movements orchestrated by the stars blowing in the wind. In 220 years, the Thousand Years of Woman and Peace will open up to receive the six thousand years of man who has been ruling the world and now is being challenged to give everything to woman.

Man is forbidden to spill his seed upon the ground but in our times, man is spilling his seed into outer space, leaving the world ransacked and broken. All the mechanization and technological advances brought about by a worldwide coalition to explore the ends of the universe while the world seethes in pain and poverty is like the Tower of Babel four thousand years ago warring against God. Humanity has been exploited for an absurdity. There is nothing in this universe like our planet Earth, Mother Earth. This errant behavior can be traced back to the Big Bang Theory and all the pernicious ramifications coming from the assumption of something out of nothing.

Coinciding with our time, the End of Days, rampant scientific discoveries from the atom to the edges of the universe are all echoing the words of זהר. Our time is a time of great global darkness when the truth is completely obscured by vulgar lies proliferating unrestrained. The knowledge of זהר a word translating as Brilliance, has come to our rescue. During the years of Rebbe Shimmon on תבל two thousand years ago, rainbows were nonexistent anywhere on the planet because the light emanating from Rebbe Shimmon as a conduit for spiritual illumination restrained the prismatic diffusion of light throughout the globe.

Though his compatriots begged him to write down the words of זהר, Rebbe Shimmon refused until the very end as chronicled in the Book זהר. Knowing the light would be too bright and would eradicate the other three levels of the Torah, Rebbe Shimmon dared not dictate a transcript into a written text during this lifetime. Plus, the knowledge of זהר, the hidden knowledge from the far side of the BlackWhole, was not pertinent to the world until now. The conclusion of the final thousand year cycle is only a couple of centuries away. The time has come to make the transition between the six thousand years of man and the long awaited for Thousand Years of Woman and Peace.

Rebbe Shimmon understood the light emanating from זהר illuminated from the other side of the BlackWhole is where the vessel and the light are One. His time on Earth was a profoundly sad time. The Second Temple was being destroyed by Rome and the Jewish People thrown out into the world to be exiled from the Land of ישראל. The Two Thousand Years of Teaching, begun when Avraham left the Tower of Babel, was ending. Beginning was the Two Thousand Years of Travail, eventually giving birth to the Thousand Years of Woman and Peace.

Knowing his generation was the wrong time to bring forth the light from זהר Rebbe Shimmon waited until after his death, recounted towards the end of the Book זהר. By incorporating his earthly conversations into his transmissions from Heaven to Earth, he was able to more easily bridge the gap. But even so, Rebbe Shimmon needed to start his transmission hundreds of years before the Book

זהר would actually become a meaningful resource for the world. That time has come, but why now? What is special about this time that זהר should be revealed?

In the summer of 2017, an eclipse of the Sun by the Moon happened across America's Bible Belt. The year was 5777 in the Hebrew calendar with only a couple of centuries left until the beginning of a new era. Trump was elected in that same year, the culmination of six thousand years was happening. The next four years were rift with lies and absurdities trying to wrest away the future in favor of the past. God judges countries by the majority and in the election of 2020 a majority of Americans voted for the future.

The past came to conclusion January 6, 2021 with the siege against the Capitol Building of the United States of America. Trump is closely connected to the 777 through his age; at the inauguration he was seventy years, seven months and seven days—this last ditch failed effort to overturn the election, was also the end of this male impurity putrefying America and therefore the world. Since America is a little world made of immigrant people from around the globe living together in peace. Now, it is incumbent on America to act; now, is the time when זהר is needed—to light the way to the future.

There is only one **אמת/Truth** but **אמת/Truth** has infinite facets. God creates and sustains creation constantly. Zohar is the pinnacle of **אמת** from where grows the infinite expressions of light obliterating the darkness and despair brought about from relying on errant belief instead of knowing. There is kindness and love flowing everywhere within everything. זהר is pertinent in our time more than another time, since instrumentation has been developed able to corroborate the ancient words from זהר. Thereby, Rome must relinquish their cold hold on reality and stop feeding the unsuspecting lies that a big bang created creation or some spiritual god did it in a blink of the eye.

Truly, there is only one choice in life. Everything stems from a wakefulness to the Creator being present for everyone all the time. The beginning of wisdom is fear; fear is a recognition of what is—one glimpse into reality and sudden change occurs. זהר comes to clarify and to prove from our own instrumentation, this is God's World and we are here to partake in pleasure within the restraints of the Seven Commandments given by בורא to all People. The Earth is a paradise ready to be enjoyed but with respect for בורא/**Creator** and for the ברה/**Creation**.

The word Covid, as in Covid-19, has three meanings in Hebrew; כבוד/**Respect**; כבוד/**Heavy**; כבוד/**Liver**. These three different meanings correspond to our thoughts, emotions and actions. The human being is judged for their intentions which are found in the head; כבוד/**Respect** stems from the head then blossoms into emotions—more evident and easier to read. Thoughts are hidden in the mind but emotions are easily shared particularly when the heart is כבוד/**Heavy**. The כבוד/**Liver** purifies the blood wherein the aspect of the soul animating the body is found. בורא is speaking to the world through the disease called, כבוד/**Covid-Respect**.

There is a web of Truth threaded through everything; since the Creator is One, the creation is also one—how each aspect of life is intertwined within an intricate array of light and darkness is far more complex than any technology could ever express. בורא sent Covid to the Earth because the world was spinning out of control, because progress had become cancerous and crazy with greed. זהר traces greed back to the Primordial Serpent who had sex with חוה/**Chava** whose original name was חיה/**Chaya-Life Giver** but later changed to חוה/**Chava** to include the חויה/**Chavia-Serpent** in Aramaic. Because of her intercourse with the חויה/**Chavia-Serpent** her name changed to חוה/**Chava**.

As a result of having sex with the serpent, she gave birth to two children: קין/**Kain-Possess** and הבל/**Hevel-Breath**. Hevel was from the seed of אדם/**Adom** and Rain from the seed of the נחש/**Serpent**. קין/**Kain** killed הבל/**Hevel** beginning ten generations of retribution ending with the Great Flood. Alma, the wife of Noah, came from the seed of Kain while her husband came from Sheth, Adom and Chava's third and final child. The three sons of Noah correlate to the three major colors: Blue/White; Green/Yellow; Red/Black who divided the world: east, west and south—Asia, Europe and Africa.

The people preceding the flood were more ephemeral, light creatures eventually toning down into color before evolving into skin. In Hebrew the word for **עור/Ore-Skin** is the same sounding word for **אור/Ore-Light**. The same sound but written differently. Every aspect of life can be unraveled with the help of **זהר** needed in our time because of the pervading darkness precludes the light. The greatest darkness is just before the dawn. Now is the time of **זהירה/Zahira-Illumination** because the greatest light comes out of the darkness like the light of the eye comes from the black of the pupil.

WHERE TO FROM HERE

We stand upon the precipice of change, of real change supplanting the paved over virtual reality of the victor's constant historical fabulation. The elaborate consortium of inherited generational lies has drained Truth from reality, a veneer of bullish excrement is all that is left. This steady diet of lies plus the constant brutalization of the individual is bad enough but proclaiming God as monotheism, inferring the highest spiritual entity, is beyond lie, it is blasphemy. The knowledge of Heaven and Earth has been filtered through the maniac ego of mercurial figures hungry for power over other people, a perception personified by the Church.

Those not mindful of God being everywhere all the time to everybody, see only themselves; all their endeavors are bleached by embarrassment from the lies they conceive—propagating false conclusions then deliberately inducing their subjects to the latest addiction. Only Truth can break through this vile veneer of vitriolic politics. Though God is not spiritual, God uses Heaven to communicate to Earth through the angels and prophets. Every people have their righteous and sages but a prophet is something different, more sublime, more connected to Heaven than to Earth. Prophesy exists across the globe and beyond boundaries.

However, there are only two books of prophesy: the Torah and the Koran. The Semitic People, the Arabs and the Jews are direct descendants from Avraham who four thousand years ago came to Earth from the Tower of Babel built on Mars. Avraham was imbued with the secret of language plus the knowledge of the 22 movements of the mouth. Avraham was able to construct a phonetic language for each son, Ishmael and Yitzchok, according to their dispositions. Ishmael was his first son born from an Egyptian princess named Hagar; he was strong bold, ruling the desert with his arrows—meaning, he was a virile man.

Arabic is an emotionally written calligraphy; a language full of intrigue—curves dancing across the page. Whereas Avraham's second son was known for his love of Truth. Yitzchok was more intellectual, thus the structure of the Hebrew language is reflected in the straight lines with little of the acrobatic maneuvers found in Arabic. These two tongues from these two sons constitute the beginning of phonetic language in the world. Later, Avraham would marry Ketora and have six sons who he sends to the East with another language but without a written form, Sanskrit. From these three fundamental Indo-European languages, the world was blessed with true prophets and wisdom books.

Prophesy can come in any language. Prophets speak the words of prophecy in an earthly language throughout the world but only the Arabs and Jews, the Semitic People, have prophetic books. The spiritual nature and singular ability of these two languages to be read on various levels of consciousness without breaking the continuity and clarity of the message is extraordinary, even wondrous. The Jewish People received the Torah 3500 years ago while the Arab People received the Koran two thousand years later. Both books come from Heaven according to the Will of God. The Torah and the Koran can stand together without contradiction, the sign of prophesy.

There was a time, three thousand years ago, when prophets proliferated the Land of Israel. There were schools for prophets and there were gangs of prophets wandering fields everywhere, throwing off their clothes, reaching states of ecstasy, drawing down wisdom clothed in words, singing and dancing as a result of prophetic visions. But, the time of the prophets has ceased for over a thousand years. Mohammad was the last prophet. Some prophets left books while other just spoke prophesy pertinent only to their generation. There are 24 Jewish books of prophesy beginning with the first Five Books of Moshe the Prophet, plus one book of Arabian lineage, the Koran from Mohammad the Prophet.

Jewish prophets were tested for their words and if found inaccurate would forfeit their lives; if the prophet proclaimed rain from sunup to sundown and the rain ended an hour before the sun set—kill the prophet because he is false. The Arab People until recently lived peaceably with the Jewish People acknowledging all the Jewish Prophets along with Mohammad the Prophet. Jesus is a Jewish prophet whose prophesy was not in his words but in his deeds. He was not crucified and did not die for anyone's sins. Dying and sins are an individual's responsibility.

The purpose of the Semitic People, the Arabs and the Jews, are to be heavenly funnels through which illumination can permeate the globe, bringing relief in the form of light. Zohar is not prophesy nor was Rebbe Shimmon ben Yichoi a prophet, rather Zohar represents the fourth level of Torah. The Written Torah is a declination of the 613 Commandments given specifically to the Jewish People. The Text hints at Laws by which to clarify and observe the 613 Commandments commanded only to the Jewish People, the Chosen People who were chosen for this purpose. Jewish Law results from the collected dialogue of the Jewish People for 1500 years before being written down two thousand years ago.

The three levels of the Oral Tradition are based upon the Talmud connecting the written words of prophesy with the Law. Spliced in amid the Law are stories, some of the stories are fantastical miraculous impossible even laughable. A well known Jewish saying, If you want to learn what to do, learn the Law, but if you want to learn the Truth about life, learn the stories, called: **אגדה/Agada-Tales**. The second level of the Oral Torah called: **Midrash/Exposition** of Law extending the path of the Law into the story until finally Zohar speaks the Truth into conversation.

The stories inspired by the Law are like the leaves of a tree alluding to a hidden fruit. The Tree of Life is rooted into the Written Torah; the trunk to the Tree of Life has limbs where the Law expands into different segments. The leaves are the Midrash and the fruit is Zohar, the third and final level of Oral Torah. Zohar is a conversation between Rebbe Shimmon and a Spanish cabalist, Moshe Shem Tov de Leon, 700 hundred years ago in Spain. Zohar is the ultimate fruit from the Tree of Life, the Light from the far side of the BlackWhole.

Though written for our time, the Light Zohar required seven hundred years of clarification, taking on physical dimension like a drop of water passing through the ground on the way to the sea. Zohar is a glimmer into the Truth but this little bit of Light is enough to brighten the entire world; a Light from beyond religion or even spirituality—a Light for the future. The darkness and lies of our time have caused Zohar to be revealed into the world for all to see the abundant knowledge and wisdom needed to correct our course through the cosmos.

The fruit on the Tree of Life has germinated inside the flower of the Cabala, key to Zohar and finally delivered to world in our time, the End of Days. The Zohar is destined to effectuate a sudden change around the globe bringing about world peace through the conservation of life on the seven continents of the Earth along with the three oceans. The fruit has at last ripened and is ready to be picked. Whoever eats from the Tree of Life will have their eyes opened, as did our primordial ancestry, the first two human beings locked within one androgynous ethereal body.

THE WAY TO PEACE

שלום/**Shalom-Peace** also means, **Whole** and **Complete**. With every division are left fractions, things that fit nowhere and only make trouble. Our world is broken and divided into political-religious boundaries oiled by titans of money. Our modern world has no purpose other than competition but for no reason and at the detriment of the world's masses while decimating the resources of the Earth. People treat the world the way they treat their own lives, get the most out of it before dying.

Only Truth has the power to forge division back into unity. There is a simple Truth which can be easily known by everyone in the world, the kernel from where all other Truths are derived—each person is equally and uniquely created. The creation of Heaven and Earth is a delicate structured full of wisdom love and illumination. Two thousand years ago, Rebbe Shimmon saw what we now see with the help of technological wizardry. Truth is corroborated by a replicated reality on all levels of existence, ubiquitously present throughout creation.

Zohar leads the way into the prophetic future, proclaiming unequivocally without any doubt or contradiction as to who our world belongs, not to man but to God. In the future, as predicted by the prophets thousands of years ago, in our time called the End of Days, each person will sit each beneath their own vine. There is a saying, The wine goes in and Truth comes out. When we each sit beneath our own vine, then the wine consumed is particular to that person and the Truth that comes out is unique. This was God's Plan at the advent of creation six thousand years ago.

During these six thousand years, the human being has gone from the captain of the ship with a God-Given power ruling the animals of the Earth, to descending through the many generations into people who are less than animals. Animals harbor an instinctive respect for life by only killing to eat, whereas human beings have the capacity to war with nature. Human history has degraded into the arrogance of the great lie perpetrated against God by proclaiming, Life just happens for no reason and will end for no reason. This kind of pernicious reasoning evokes fear from asteroids slamming into the Earth killing everything or aliens coming down to eat us alive in a world completely devoid of compassion.

The structure derived from the Tree of Life is the Signature of the Creator permeating every design. How to serve the Creator is an individual choice. There are many wisdom traditions to garner advice and direction but there is no obligation other than the Seven Commandments and what each person takes upon themselves in their own personal relationship with the Creator. The Jewish People were given the Torah to bring the light to the world proclaiming, God is One. God is everywhere to everyone all the time. This is the original message conveyed to the Earth by Avraham and later twisted by religion into monotheism.

Millennium of religious dogma coupled with governmental rule and scientific endeavor has cordoned the power to enslave humanity for a singular purpose benefitting the highest of the elite. The lie is vulnerable to Truth because immense amounts of darkness are dispelled with a tiny ray of light. The secret of light is in being tied to the source and never separated. The Creator is the source of light and life equally to all. No one can horde the light. Social inequalities are purposely place in critical aspects of life to maintain control.

Treating the Earth with proper respect will help to realign our world as a healer might realign the bones of the body to help the sinews and the muscles come back to center. The powers ripping the world apart are trying to spin her out of control until she is drunk with excess and readied for the rape. They use flagrant fake philosophical excuses perpetrating their dogmatic view on the rest of the globe. After communism and capitalism, comes cooperation working together as one unified world in pursuit of balance, regulated by moderate social restrictions maintaining law enforced by timely justice.

The world is meant to acknowledge the Creator and live under the decree of the King to do the Seven Commandments given to the first human being, male and female, for their progeny throughout these six thousand years. Having social restrictions and courts of law are essential to keeping a balanced society. In ancient times, cops were used to carry out the sentence of the court, not to prevent crime. In a balanced society there is little motive for crime. The lies of politics are well known, the lies of religion and authority are less apparent but just as lethal, perhaps more.

Society will change because that is God's Will but how society changes is up the eight billion people who populate the world. Zohar comes to illuminate the future upon tendrils freshly sprouted from the Tree of Life. However, before any of this can happen, war must cease throughout the world. Most wars are sectarian wars brought on by the religious divisions often within the same religion. Many religious wars carry on for centuries. Some wars are territorial or resource based but the father of all wars comes out of the Middle East—when war stops in the Middle East, war will cease in the world.

ENDING WAR

The divide between the Arab and Jewish worlds can never be bridged without first solving the Palestinian Problem. The Palestinian People were living on the Promised Land when Avraham arrived in the year two thousand, beginning the Two Thousand Years of Teaching. Throughout the world during this time, great teachers arose venerated until today. Both Avraham and his two sons made covenants with the Palestinian People to forever live together in peace. This covenant must be abided by. Without rectifying this injustice, there can never be peace in the Middle East nor in the world. But there is a solution, a very simple solution.

Ben Laden is named in Zohar called Baladen, described as subhuman, a dog coming to drink the blood after the lion has departed. And so it was, Saddam Hussein known as the Lion of Babylon lost his country to the invading Roman Army spurred on from the State of

Israel fearing direct confrontation with Iraq. Israel had always fought their own wars up until America invaded and destroyed Iraq, adding to what would become a twenty year war in Afghanistan while continuing decades long hostilities with Iran. But, it was Baladen who carried forward the banner of blood.

Middle Eastern hatred for the State of Israel is founded from the Jewish Diaspora who began returning to Israel a hundred and fifty years ago. Their ancient home Israel had been the place of two Temples, each lasting more than four hundred years until destroyed by Babylon and Rome, on the same day, the Ninth of Av five hundred years apart. When the Jews returned, they brought with them the infidelities from the West plus a penchant for power. Having lived mostly in Europe, the Zionists who came to Israel over a century ago knew how to acquire money and deal in western politics. The Arabs saw this intrusion as the point of the Roman spear. In the subsequent years, that spear has only gotten longer and sharper.

When Clinton put the first American base in Saudi Arabia, Baladen announce his war against the West; he went to Afghanistan to build an army pitting the Koran against the Bible, bringing disgrace upon God for using the Koran as a weapon. Clinton laughed when he heard the news that Baladen had declared war on America because to knew how much money a new war would fill the coffers for American excess. Vietnam had been a disaster but everyone had made a lot of money. America is economically based in war, needing war to survive.

For years, the temperature was being ramped up in the Middle East eventually leading to the inevitable, a pretense for war. America's response was not one of revenge but rather a justification to completely reconstruct world power, since the West held leverage. World War One was expanded to give time for the conquest of the Middle East, their hidden agenda. These Masters of War have a map to where they are going; they play current events like they play the stock market— money and power is their objective. Rome who lives by the sword pays for war with the Roman coin.

I was born in 1944, between D-Day, the end of the Second World War in Europe, and the atomic bomb dropped on Japan a year later. I was on the ship that started the Vietnam War and saw before my very eyes the perpetrated lie. And all who died as a result of that lie left a skewed history written by these vicars of wealth. I was four when Israel became a state. Many devout Jewish people thought it a mistake to declare Israel a separate State entity from the Arabs, even though the Arabs had supported the Nazis during the war, but statehood won out.

As a result of the Jewish State, the Palestinians were eventually squeezed from the land, then herded into camps; the Gaza Strip was the only place they could call home—though living on the land continuously for four thousand years. They were now excluded from the land, like the Kurds in the north, an even more ancient people who had been the original occupants of Iran. Both Avraham and his son Yitzchok took refuge with the Palestinians and even made covenants to forever live together on the land but the Jewish State made that impossible. The Arabs had taken all of the Middle East, the Jews had taken the Land of Israel and the Palestinians had the tiny Gaza Strip.

The Palestinians did not have the pedigree of Arab, but shared Islam in common through their connection to the Koran. The Palestinians were used as the Arab weapon to fight against the Israeli State after Arab armies were unable to conquer the Jews. Some in Israel said, The Arabs will fight to the last drop of Palestinian blood. During the Yom Kippur War of 1973, the Jewish State took the Sinai up to the Suez Canal preventing world shipping. As a result of taking the Sinai, they also inherited the Palestinian problem. Through a land grab, Egypt had taken the Sinai to stage wars against Israel, now they had lost the Sinai.

Egypt had previously fenced off the Gaza Strip, restricting travel to Palestinians who had been reduced to workers, a once proud people were now slaves to Jews and Arabs alike. When Israel won the Yom Kippur War, they were left with the Gaza Strip to administer. The West was using Israel as a weapon against the Arabs, who in turn, used the Palestinians as thorn in the eye of Israel. Rome had managed to divide and conquer, incurring incalculable amount of suffering throughout the Middle East and the world but thereby became a super power.

Eventually, Israel gave back the Sinai, which had never been a part of the ancient Jewish inheritance, for a peace treaty with Egypt who took back the Sinai until today. The solution seems obvious: repay the Palestinians for this injustice by giving them the Sinai for their nation, a place contiguous with Gaza plus full of natural resources able to support the entire vastness of this area powered by the Sun. Certainly, many nations will want to come and help make the new Palestine the most modern country in the world. A once proud people has been humbled, the time has come for a righteous restitution.

Moshe 3500 years ago led the Jewish People to the land promised to Avraham who bequeathed the land to his son Yitzchok, blessing his son Yaakov with the land and the obligation to do the 613 Commandments, many of which can only be done on the Land of Israel. The Canaanites who lived on the land were given the choice: leave, become slaves or die in battle. But, though a fierce people as described in the Torah, the Palestinians were left on the land to live together with the Jews. It is incumbent upon the Semitic People, Arab and Jew, to see this wrong is made right.

LION LAMB PIG

Our planet is named Tavel, with a gematria of 432 the same as the 432 hertz resounding from the ground. Tavel is also a term for man or woman having sex with an animal. The human being is a combination of a human soul trapped inside an animal body. The animal is transgender because flesh loves flesh but the human is more discriminating. Many human habits are mimicked by the animals like cats cleaning themselves or the masked raccoons stealing away in the night; some people roar like a lion while others are impervious like the bear—we are the human animal made from clay able to articulate thoughts into speech.

Every person portrays a particular type of animal, giving personality along with vitality for the human soul used in expression. Also, countries and regions around the globe have animal representations like: America is the Eagle flying above all other nations; the Middle East is the lion; Russia the Bear; Asia the Dragon. Rome is the Pig. One day the Arab Lion will lie down with the Jewish Lamb and there will be peace in the world. But before any of that can happen, the Pig must first return. In Hebrew, the Pig is called חזיר/**Chazir-Return** because one day the Pig will return to God and become kosher.

The Semitic People, the Arab and the Jew, abhor Pig. In the Torah, while describing which animals are kosher, the Text stops to give special attention to the Pig who is the only animal in the world displaying one sign of kosher, cloven hooves, but not the other sign of kosher, multiple stomachs. Kosher fish have fins and scales and in the whole world, there is no fish displaying scales without fins or fins without scales. Also, all kosher mammals display both cloven hooves with multiple stomachs. The Pig is the only animal in the world having cloven hooves but only one stomach. This fact begs to be interpreted.

The camel is one of the three animals in the world having multiple stomachs but not cloven hooves. The camel sleeps with his hooves curled beneath least his non-kosher self be revealed, but the Pig is the opposite, known for splaying out their legs while sleeping. The Pig is the sign of a hypocrite, on the outside is kosher but within is impure. Rome is depicted in the Talmud as a Pig with a golden ring through his nose. Pigs are led by their nose through the mechanism of a ring. Meaning, Rome follows the money. Rome is famous for their coin and their sword, but mostly for their religion. And Pigs love the mud.

Religion was invented by Rome, displaying the cross everywhere along with their lying book the Bible replete with a story about how a Jewish Rabbi is god and how the Jewish People are forever cursed for having caused the cruel death of Jesus, until this day suffering nailed to a cross. There is not one shred of historical evidence that Jesus even lived; only through the Koran is Jesus known but there is no cross—the Roman story is a complete fabrication, a blood libel. The Pig is a liar and a hypocrite portending righteousness and authority.

The time has come to take Jesus down from the cross, beginning Rome's return back to God who is everywhere all the time to everyone. Yet, through their religion, plus their obsession conquering the globe, the message of Moshiach has spread throughout the world, even though everything the Bible says is an outright lie. Moshiach is not a lie and Rome can not kill Moshiach by torturing a Jewish rabbi; even though the rabbis might deserve some torturing for leading the Jewish People astray, off the path of Torah—like the Church, the rabbis have adopted religion, using Moshiach to make money.

Moshiach is a gift from God, a beautiful human soul waiting at the foot of God's Throne for six thousand years; destined to descend from Heaven to Earth when world-wide peace is achieved—to be crowned King over the Jewish People. Rome concocted their lie then scratched together bits and pieces of the Truth to sweeten the lie making it palatable. Religion is synonymous with lying because anyone purporting to know anything beyond physical and spiritual is a liar. Religion with their dogma, more than anything else in the world, has dumbed down the human being, making a mockery of ancient texts and ways.

Every year the earthquakes come closer to the Vatican, the only country in the world with zero population growth, the nation of Amalek who must be destroyed before God's Name is Whole. God proclaims in the Torah כי מחה אמחה את זכר עמלק מתחת השמים/**I will destroy the memory of Amalake from beneath the heavens**. Another vision of the future predicts, Rome will be left with one crumbling wall. The Lion will lie down with the Lamb, the Pig will return and the Bear, the Dragon and the Eagle will show mutual respect for each other. Then the world will be at peace; then God's gift to the world can descend—then, Moshiach will come floating down to the Earth for all to see.

However, first the Jew must be taken down from the cross. This terrible travesty, this racist display is more egregious than anything in the world;

it must come to an end, along with the Roman calendar and the naming of the planets according to ancient Roman mythology. Roman religion is as true as the mythology they proclaim. Rome lives by the lie, the outer appearance of kosher while harboring impure intentions within. All the ways of Rome lead to war. Religious wars, fighting over a lie, oppressing people to accept the lie and build society around the lie until the lie becomes the truth.

The Light Zohar illuminates the Truth while annihilating the Big Bang Theory and other detrimental speculative ideas, yet religion is the source of all lies. Religion is not respected in Heaven being completely devoid of light. People are leaving religion in droves. Religion must be irradiated before peace can reign in the world. Religion can be easily dismantled by forcing them to pay taxes on their vast empire of land and businesses. There is no place for religion in this world; people placing themselves between the person and their Creator—Christianity is racist, down to their core, forcing people to bow down to the White Man while scapegoating the Jew.

The Bible is a filthy rendition of a blatant lie. The Bible should be thrown into the crematoriums and burnt into ashes like I was for being a Jew.

Rome is destined to return to the fold of human compassion giving thanks to the Creator for the great kindness of precious life. Zohar destroys the lie but not the liar who is left in the darkness and emptiness of their pitiful lives until forced by the world around them to finally return back to the Creator in repentance. With religion gone, the light and love of life will quickly return and the world will revive, as the future awakens within the heart of each person. This is not a pipe dream, this is prophesy about to happen in our time.

THE LAND OF ISRAEL

The Torah, written from Heaven 3500 years ago, establishes the boundaries to the Land of Israel that are clearly delineated in the Text. This delineation is important since many of the 613 Commandments given to the Jewish People can only be done while living on the land, no matter what nation controls the land. But, why is the Land of Israel so important? Why not somewhere else on the Earth? The first human being was made from the dust of the Earth gathered to the Land of Israel to be constructed and eventually buried in the Caves of Hebron, one of the four holy cities in the Land of Israel, corresponding to the element of earth.

There are four ancient cities in Israel corresponding to the four elements: חברון/**Chevron-Earth** where the first couple is buried; ירושלים/**Yerushiliam-Fire** where within the Temple sacrifices were offered; קינרית/**Kinneret** (Harp)-**Water** where the inland sea is formed like a harp; צפת/**Sfat-Air** hovering above the Harp Sea in the high mountains in the north where Rebbe Shimmon who authored Book Zohar, is interned. Within the dimensions to the Land of Israel, the ground must be rested every seven years and after seven cycles the land reaches Jubilee, returning back to the original owners. Trees are forbidden to be harvested for the first three years after planting. Both Temples were built on the Land of Israel.

Perhaps the most persuasive argument for the Land of Israel is being situated in the Middle East. The globe is made in a human form composed in seven segments: brains—Scandinavia; chest—Europe and Asia; arms sunken in the oceans, hands—Britain and Japan; legs—Africa and South America; Canada—back; America—buttocks, seat of power; Ovaries of Mother Earth—Australia and New Zealand; Sex—Mediterranean Sea; place of conception—Israel.

The Land of Israel is called the Promised Land, promised to the Jewish People who are the Chosen People, chosen to do the 613 Commandments which we have continuously observed for 3500 years, through five exiles: Egypt, Babylon, Persia, Greek and Rome. The exile of Rome, by far the longest exile, has been ongoing for two thousand years, since Rome burned down the Second Temple which had stood in Jerusalem for 420 years. The First Temple had stood in the same place for 410 years before being destroyed by Babylon. The Jewish People have remained devout throughout, the Chosen

People seeking their Promised Land in a circuitous path across the narrow bridge above an endless abyss.

Zohar predicts: In the End of Days, the tribe of Rueben will return to the Land, take the Land by invoking terror throughout the world and will eventually win, but they will not remain because they came for the wrong reason. There is no question, this is referring to the Zionists who came to Palestine, a Roman name change indicating a loss of Jewish Land, seeking refuge from the Roman stigma perpetrated by the religious dogma that the Jews had killed god, a Jewish rabbi named Jesus. This false, villainess libelous concoction has decimated the Jewish People.

In a world of eight billion, after four thousand years, the Jewish People are less than twenty million strong, half of whom live in Israel, a refuge for the Jewish People. By adopting governmental norms over ancient Jewish obligation, Israel became a state. Israel is a refuge from the antisemitism perpetrated by this lie of deicide yet this secular occupation of the Land Promised to the Chosen People is a land usurped. Infested with Western Religion, repugnant to our Arab Brothers who already suspect the Jewish State of funneling Western ideas into the Middle East is a Land sacred to Arabs. Israel is forever under siege from the entire world. This prediction from Zohar ends by saying, they won but they will not remain.

Throughout the world, Rome with their Western Civilization has pushed their agenda everywhere with one common denominator, devoted to keeping power at any cost. Yet, Roman rule has also invented new ways, adapting to difficulties with unique solutions brought about by creative minds producing remarkable innovations. We have the capacity to make the world a better place for all human beings whose image is drawn from the Tree of Life, configured into the form of the YHVH. The time has come to awake from the nightmare of exile and to embrace the light of redemption coming to the world for all to partake.

The Land of Israel needs to prepare for the coming of the Third Temple, descending from the heavens, made of indestructible material, never to be destroyed. The End of Days means, the end of the six thousand year male agenda and instead embrace of the coming Thousand Years of Woman and Peace—שבת/**Shabbat-Rest** to the world. These next two centuries are the transition between male dominance prior to the celestial merging of male into female. The dogmatic thinking of the past has insnared many unsuspecting victims, blinded into pointless warriors bowing down to false gods pushing vile lies.

Dogma is the biggest impediment to freedom from Rome. Jewish dogma is found in the rabbi's insistence for obedience to Rabbinic Law. Rabbinic Law was made by the Rabbis as a clear example of how to live the Torah in a consistent manner in all aspects of life. However, the obligation to observe these laws are clearly only on the rabbis. The way of Torah is peace and freedom. The rabbis have robbed peace and freedom from the Jewish People by instituting themselves as a final authority by making Rabbinic Law obligatory upon the Jewish People, rendering them guilty before God. But, there is something deeper.

There will never be peace in the Middle East until the rabbis acknowledge the validity of the Koran. To be a Muslim one must believe in the Prophet Mohammad and his prophesy the Koran. This acknowledgement in no way diminishes the Jewish People but rather strengthens our connection to our Arab brothers. Rabbinic Law is the strictest of all law but to exclude our brothers and cause forever war is too strict.

u

Chapter Nine

RAMIFICATIONS

The four levels of the Torah: the Written Word with the three Oral Traditions written down two thousand years ago: Talmud/Law; Midrash/Story; Zohar/Brilliance are comparable to the four elements: fire, air, water, earth. The Earth is the Written Torah comprised of 24 prophetic books inscribed forever never to be altered, but the three levels of Oral Torah are ephemeral, changing throughout generations without incurring contradiction to the Written Word. Revealing the element of fire through זהר divulges the soul of creation reaching into every facet into the jewel of life.

Science has recently come to acknowledge, what they identify as Dark Matter scattered in clumps throughout the universe as a fifth dimension, and they are right. In the East, this fifth dimension is called Ether and in the West is called Soul. Astronomers probing the universe have been able to identify features of spirituality, an existence without corporeality. Zohar opens up and illuminates the factual evidence gathered by science by giving purpose to every aspect of creation. Beneath the stern glare of Zohar, religion melts back into the dark recesses of ignorance and manipulation. Only Truth can stand before Zohar.

The ramifications to Zohar after being refined over the last thousand years has produced an amazing fruit able to overcome the senses by shaking awake those too tired to be illuminated. Frustration and bitterness is fueling a nihilistic future where only the very few at the top survive. Zohar was prepared for our time, the End of Days when the whole world as one, decides on the future. There is proof to the Truth corroborated by empirical investigation, while the lie waits in the shadows ready to strike at any moment of indecision or doubt.

Zohar brings forth the knowledge embedded in the Light from behind the BlackWhole; Zohar is an aggressive light, eating up the darkness of doubt, obliterating the unnatural confinement produced from dogma—Zohar frees the human spirit. Servitude to false gods will become impossible as the Light ramps up from the revelation of the fifth dimension, the spiritual ether wherein the soul is embedded reaching out to Earth connecting to every bit of existence. Each tiny mosquito in the countless swarms of mosquitos or bedbugs are each one precious to the Creator. God is Great and there is nothing in creation which is superfluous.

The ramifications to Zohar being revealed in this time challenges religion and science to prove their errant theories and fabricated fallacious assumptions before the glare of Brilliance. Zohar illuminates our world for all to see the symmetry of life depicted and refracted throughout the universe from the lowest creature to the highest heights. The time is running out to chose God before God becomes completely self-evident to everyone on the planet. God's desire to be known in low is only fulfilled through the human being wheeling freedom of choice. Soon the Light will be too strong, obliterating choice, completely.

We must teach our children the Truth and free the human soul to love without fear of retribution. The lie is beginning to unravel, glints of light are peeking through the crumbling veneer of falsehoods. The Torah begins with the letter **ב/Bet** with a gematria of two, indicating this is the second world of creation in our solar system. The first world was the interior of Mars, a water world full of kindness where independence reigned supreme. There, woman was made. The interior of our world is fire, the second branch on the Tree of Life is גבורה/ **Gevorah-Severity**.

Ours is a hard and difficult world made harder by man's insistence. Zohar comes at a time when the severity needs to be sweetened. The three letters in the name **אדם/Adom** can rearranged to מאד/ **Moad-More**. Man naturally wants more, but just as the left foot restrains the right foot from going out too far, so too does woman restrain man's focus, turning his will. Together we can navigate our world to a new paradigm, the coming Thousand Years of Woman and Peace. The words of Zohar come to soothe the sorrowed soul for the mistakes the body has endured.

Zohar comes to purge, just as the epidemic Covid, a word in Hebrew meaning Respect, sweeps across the globe stopping the frantic pace of a world about to spin out of control. Those wanting to rule the world know how to exploit chaos; the global bandits know how to turn people into slaves—a well practiced dance for millennium. The Light Zohar from the other side of the BlackWhole illuminates while demanding כבוד/**Covid-Respect**. Every person in this world should bend the knee to the Creator in simple acknowledgement and thanks to the Creator and Sustainer of creation.

Light illuminates but Respect demands humility. Love and Respect are the right and left Hands of God holding humanity close. The lies melt away beneath the Light. Those perpetrating the demand for more will slink away humiliated. Soon in the future, there will be a clear declination between the dark side with a hidden agenda and the bright side of life. Teaching our children throughout the world to seek the light makes the world brighter. This second cycle of life does not need and was never meant by the Creator to be this hard. This is too hard.

The ramifications of revealing the secret of Zohar in our time is significant. Once released, the antidote to the sickness plaguing the world, nothing can stop the spread of Truth which will eat up the darkness for breakfast. This process is undefinable by creed, doctrine or dogma, as the Creator of this phantasmagorical creation is unknowable by the puny human intellect or highest level of spiritual cognition. The best we can do, like a cow staring at the moon fascinated by the light, wondering what it is? God wants to be known in low; we are the lowest generation just prior to the culmination—time has come to know the Creator of creation.

SCIENCE MUST ADAPT

Authority is dangerous and often leads to a dogmatic subservience to the leader and a belief in the power of man. There needs to be an authority and there needs to be leaders but there is no need for the dogma demanded by the authority. Dogma insists in truths without proof, only on the word of the authority or leader. Authority is founded in the ego of man whose nature is to go out and explore the mysteries of life. Women are more prone to staying within, nurturing life. Science is a male attribute.

Male and female are equal sides to the human being but going in different directions, man going out and woman going in. Plus, these six thousand years which end in 220 years are dedicated to the perfecting of man by woman. The equality of woman in the workplace has only changed society for the better by helping man to mature in anticipation of merging into the Thousand Years of Woman and Peace. Science, academia and religion are the three most formidable ego driven disciplines demanding obedience from the flock. Both science and religion make themselves the authority on reality; academia fosters politics which is the science of the lie—while science views reality from the perspective of earthly intellect.

From our place on Earth, science determines how to view reality; though we see only the four elemental building blocks: earth, water, air, fire—science builds a different model with over a hundred elements only they can recognize, annotated with mysterious letters and numbers in a secretive cabal suited for the intellectual elite. Instead of the four levels of human experience, science only acknowledges three states of matter: physical, aquatic and gaseous. In 1939, the beginning of World War Two, science struck another blow against reality by changing the standard measurement for music from 432 hertz to 440 hertz. The Earth resonates at 432 hertz, the gematria of **תבל/Earth**.

More recently, science downgraded the planet Pluto, thereby leaving only eight planets. The nine planets plus the Sun equal ten, as in the

עשר ספירות/**Ten Sefirot-Luminaries** to the Tree of Life portrayed in the ten fingers and toes. Science sees chaos but finds only order. Whenever science rips at the fabric of nature something diabolical emerges from cold facts, like the atom bomb. The ego of man has yet to be cowed by the Creator. Man has a theory, the Big Bang Theory, where something comes from nothing, order from disorder. Life suddenly emerges from chaos, including aliens and monsters.

These rampantly ridiculous absurd pernicious ideas should be hung by the neck until dead. A more nihilistic theory has never been composed, harboring hidden deleterious effects on the human psyche. Inflicting the human mind with these absurd ideas, these baneful braggadocios bullish excrement is completely beyond belief, yet people believe. The human being is vulnerable, easily seduced and manipulated. Having been barred from Heaven by religion, the vulnerable human being looks to science whose undeniable facts are forced to fit into errant theories which have a subtle way of skewing the Truth, leaving the believer of such absurdities in dire danger of depression.

Only the Truth can turn the oceanic tide against these false gods who steal from Heaven in an attempt to rule the Earth. This is why Zohar was meant for our time, as absolute proof there is observable structure present throughout the universe, an irrefutable design from the Creator who created creation through a logic begetting cause and effect. The religious idea of creation instantaneously being born out of nothing is as detrimental to the human spirit as is the Big Bang Theory where something comes out of nothing. God wants to be acknowledge for creating creation and also being constantly involved in every aspect of creation at every moment in time.

Time is plotted by science as an incremental line adapted to the Roman religion but time is not a line, rather a spiral coming to conclusion, now in the End of Days when the six thousand years of male endeavor merges with the coming Thousand Years of Woman and Peace. Prophets throughout the globe, particularly the prophetic books, the Torah and the Koran, is what keeps the human spirit tethered to Heaven. Authorities demanding respect by imposing obedience place themselves between the Truth and the people in much the same way politicians are impositions in democracy.

Science must adapt to the Truth. God is not spiritual nor physical, there is nothing God cannot do, nothing is out of reach of the Creator who creates moment by moment to fulfill the primordial desire to be known in the depths of time and space, on a little chunk of rock taken from beneath the Throne of the King of Creation, building a pebble into our world then placing the Earth precisely so the Moon would perfectly eclipse the Sun in a miracle of nature. We believe what we do not know; those unaware of the Truth—believe in something else.

Children need to be taught the Truth, not some scientific religious bullish excrement based on theories or lies. From the onset of a child's first innocent question, Where are we? Children should be taught the Truth. The Creator created Heaven and Earth by engraving into the Name of God who regulates nature into a glowing illumination beyond Heaven. We are surrounded by the Light and Love of the Creator and when you are alone, talk to the Creator who is always listening. If this were the message to our children, each unique life would be easier on planet Earth.

In 1999 I wrote a short manuscript based on my studies in the Tree of Life, explaining why astronomers would eventually discover five moons around the planet Pluto. Seven years later they made such a proclamation and recently flew by for corroboration. Zohar written two thousand years ago stands at the fulcrum of discovery, no theories should be considered valid without the validation of Book Zohar, a knowledge from an unknowable light existing prior to creation on the other side of the BlackWhole. The greatest light comes from the darkest place illuminating the gloominess of our time during this climatic moment in human history.

PROGRESS IS A CANCER

Some want to define the human experience according to our industry, even going so far as claiming our superiority comes from the function of our hands able to do intricate work. Yet, the human being is unable to engineer like a beaver with branches or from trigs perfect smoothness like the inside of a humming bird's nest. The human ability outpacing most animals is our skill at adaptation, this more than any other physical trait has allowed the human specie to persist. However, without a cogent idea of why creation exists, the human being is destined to be manipulated into another's scheme in the race to excess.

World economics is based on convincing the populous to live in excess, having too many things resulting from an unbridled desire fueled from greed. Our disposable culture is clogged with garbage. America has grown fat with the excess of wealth in blatant disregard to the sufferings from the rest of the world; we have become despicable in our own eyes—yet, America is setting the bar to progress beyond what is even possible to attain. Offering up fables based on Roman gods transformed through modernization into aliens, while the world is being despoiled. Our attention is purposely being distracted into an outer space, a place void of reality, as if this is our mission in life to forge blindly forth.

There is no point in going into outer space other than to invent new technological toys which have little or no application on the Earth. This high priced game plus the pernicious nature of progress is polluting our planet. The Torah prophesies that in the future, the world will be covered with inequities causing the heavens to sweat lead. As a result of the last fifty years in space, the accumulated space junk is beginning rain down upon the world with catastrophic results. Space junk burning up during reentry is misleading. Metal is reduced down to tiny particulates which eventual descend into the clouds mixing with the water vapor producing toxic rain.

A Hard Rain is falling upon the Earth through putrid skies into foul waters feeding our plants for human consumption. Progress has not been focused on human betterment but has instead become a metastasizing cancer consuming the consumer. After the Jewish People built the Golden Calf, Moshe took the idol and crushed the thing into dust then mixed the powder with drinking water to test the people. Those who were guilty died. But in our time when we all guilty of this horrible excess, the false god of technology has transformed into a rampant plague disregarding the innocent. Progress can not keep up with the cancer because progress is a cancer. The technology that cures cancer just makes more cancer.

Technology has extended the vapid lives of the rich yet those championing progress have no reason to live, a product of negative thinking brought on by the Big Bang Theory promoting technology as the ultimate human advancement aimed at overcoming nature. This vain pursuit to war against God is just plain stupid. People dream of making our solar system imbued with human intelligence but God is way ahead. From the beginning of creation, God set a plan for our solar system consisting of seven cycles of seven thousand years on each of the outer seven planets. Earth is 5780 years into the second of these seven thousand year cycles. The first cycle was on Mars.

Were it that instead of teaching our children about the Big Bang Theory aliens and nihilism, we taught them instead how creation is held in the hands of the Creator between absolute zero and the speed of light; and how all the light in the heavens is tethered to the Earth—the lowest place in creation where each human being is privileged to live for decades before returning to Heaven where the soul, which is engraved out of a star, will be rewarded for a life of kindness well-lived.

The final reward in physical life is to hear the angels applaud as we lift off from the Earth when our time has expired. Our world is a narrow entranceway into the main Hall in Heaven; if every day is the final day, then it does not matter how long you live but how well you live—our actions in this world are the predicate to our station in the next world. Just as there is no day without a night, also birth to death is only half the circle of life, returning back to Heaven completes the cycle. Zohar proclaims, If a person lives a thousand years is this world, looking back after death will appear as one day in the celestial years embedded into infinity.

Chapter Ten

THE FUTURE

Now, that the true meaning of Zohar has been revealed in the world, what happens next. Like the vaccine which can cure the sick and prevent illness, Zohar has the capacity to radically change society by exposing the Truth: God is the Creator of Heaven and Earth. Not only is God the Creator of creation but God is forever creating and destroying to guide existence with an ethereal hand. For those with eyes wide-open, the text can be read and easily understood, but not for those lured asleep by the menacing manipulating manmade academic-religious-scientific institutions, they need a helping hand.

God's Hand is constantly sweeping across creation while the human being signs back. Some hold their hands to their hearts in prayer while others clinch their fists to fight, to fight against God. Throughout the centuries of Jewish history there has always been an enemy wanting to wipe out the Jews thus stop God's Plan. The Jewish People performing the 613 Commandments are as essential to the world as is the wind pushing the spiraled history of the world forward. The Creator has structured creation allowing freedom of choice to the individual yet retains control by tying all endeavors to God's Will.

No one can divert God's Plan for creation but what human free choice can do is be part of the story by acknowledging the Plan and wanting to play a part. God finds great interest in each human story and God's Desire to be known in low is momentarily satisfied by an endless array of unimpressive people to all but God. Truly, no one knows what is pleasing in the eye of the Creator and therefore great care should be taken for each person. All are precious before God. Children are celebrated coming into the world but only the rich and powerful are celebrated when leaving the world, as if life is a competition and they had won.

I was once privileged to be amid a small group of street people who were sporadically gathering in a field where a compatriot was passing away. The air around the man was thick with mystery and those who gathered were strident in their solemnity, recognizing an ancient rite of passage was happening before their astounded eyes. Elsewhere, people were dying in antiseptic hospital beds lashed to the expediency of capitalism to digest whatever is left of an accumulated wealth gathered through a lifetime. God is present in both scenarios; death is inevitable but the question is—who will be embarrassed in Heaven?

The greatness of Zohar is the illuminating simplicity of life; life ain't that hard, we make it hard, we make life impossible—even the rich of richest suffer. There are many natural obstacles in life placed by the Creator for the benefit of human evolution toward a more perfect person but those obstacles placed by the opposition represent a more difficult situation. Often times God is called upon by an entire nation to help stem the tide, like the recent racist uprising. Racists are people who know nothing about God, who think the Creator of creation, Heaven and Earth is spiritual. Better they were never born.

A door in Heaven has been opened by Zohar revealing more than any scientific discovery, more than any ancient artifact or modern theory; Zohar opens a door changing everything—challenging all accepted norms, an iconoclastic work of pure light. If a disease can suddenly ravage the world so can the Truth. No person is needed, no leader is required because Truth is ubiquitously present in each personal journey through life. Life is meant to be a unique experience not something preplanned for expediency benefiting only the wealthy. The question is, where do we go from here?

The key to the future is woman. All human beings are composed in different degrees of male and female energy thus giving the experience of transgender but only woman is made to give birth, the sign of infinity. Where the other nine components to the Tree of Life point, the tenth component known as מלכות/**Malkut-Royalty** turns as depicted by the tenth celestial body. The Sun and eight planets all stay within their specified orbits but Pluto, the tenth celestial body turns into Neptune's orbit for twenty years out of the 248 year orbit around the Sun, last occurring in 1999.

Women are emerging into places of power with a different agenda for the world. Many men welcome the change and are in complete support. The world is naturally transitioning from being a male oriented world to elevating woman above man; the Thousand Years of Woman and Peace are rushing towards the Earth while the world travails prior to the eminent end of the male agenda—instead, the focus needs to be on the wants of woman. When women are happy, men are happy. The Earth is pregnant with these final 220 year; Earth is ready to give birth any moment to a future so new—as if suddenly come down from Heaven.

Time has come to shed the Skin of the Serpent, the hiss of religion, the bite of usury and the venom unleashed by the superpower of ego who have controlled the story of humanity. But now, the cat is out of the bag. There is no question, the human being has shown ourselves in every corner of the world to be worthy and good, flowing with compassion and industry. We are all the same, just different aspects contained within the first human being disseminated throughout the generations coming to conclusion in our time according to the many signs happening around the globe.

By illuminating the structure of creation, Zohar obliterates errant theories meant to emasculate male primacy, weakening the individual for the purpose of a manufactured reality while abandoning uniqueness. But time has run out, the system meant to produce more has stopped and the time is ripe to envision a new world both physically and spiritually without the intervention of dictum and dogma. Reality is a conglomerate of human experience caught in the ebb and flow of time, reduced down into a spiral. Every moment in life is a profound honor.

CONCLUSION

What is the Truth? The only Truth that really matters is the clear understanding that God who is neither physical nor spiritual, created the world and continues sustaining and watching over the Earth. This is the genesis of choice, everything else just follows. Zohar comes at the End of Days to illuminate without any doubt the structure of the universe at a time when technology allows the descriptions found in Zohar to be corroborated by scientific fact. The Light Zohar comes from the inside of the BlackWhole illuminating the end of the six thousand year cycle, when the darkness is palpable.

Once clearly established in the psyche of man, that God is all the time everywhere to everyone constantly creating creation, then freedom choice becomes a dance with God. This singular clarity is the basis for all subsequent choices; all choices are ultimately a choice about God—when God is acknowledged as partner in life then life transforms into purpose. Even when the thief enters in to steal, first he prays to God for success from the same God who forbids stealing. Only by acknowledging the Creator can change happen. The reverberations from this primal acknowledgement inculcate everywhere in every action with the intention of serving the Creator, each in a unique way yet with an inclusiveness into the whole from where we emerged from the BlackWhole.

The prophesy of the future maintains, Everyone will sit beneath their own vine and teachers will no longer be necessary. When the world acknowledges the reason for creation, fulfilling God's Desire to be known in low, then the importance each person plays in the enactment towards fulfilling God's Desire will be recognized and respected. What could be more purposeful than fulfilling God's Desire? Science obscures the Truth; religion skews the Truth—everyone else sells the Truth. The essential action required is, acknowledging the simple ubiquitous Truth. A world tethered to Truth can never go far astray.

Through brains and braun fueled by the human spirit, the six thousand years dedicated to the refinement of man is coming to a close, like a book whose story is about to conclude resolving the disparate plot threads and unanswered questions. Only now can we look back on six thousand years of human history and make a determination as to what is happening and where we go from here. What is the future for planet Earth and the human specie? What does life mean and where is life going? These unanswered questions beg for resolution.

Just as Zohar clearly delineates the segmentations of the past, so too does the text give reference to the future and to the scope of creation by explaining, The Creator made creation spectacularly vast, as to marvel the eye of man seen from a tiny point enmeshed within a cloud of stars peeking out from behind the black pupil of a human eye in wonderment. Every human life on Earth begins with a wide-open eyed wonderment of the newborn. At first the child can only see as far as the nipple but as life expands, so does vision.

After six thousand years, human vision has expanded to the outer reaches of the universe, 14 billion light years and surveyed countless stars mapping possible planets for life but nothing has been found or will be found. Another lie perpetrated by people unaware of the Creator. This malicious lie is founded on supposition, If life happened once in one place in the universe then certainly if must have happened somewhere else, according to probability. This basic assumption, taught in schools to our children is polluting their young minds along with religious dogma.

Their scientific logical premise is incorrect because life did not just happen, rather we are the culmination of God's Celestial Plan to be known in low. After all these male suppositions, like a man walking around in the dark refusing directions wanting rather to figure it out by casting himself headlong into the mirror of his own ego scattering into sharp shards throughout the globe until it becomes impossible to walk the Earth without getting cut, what now?

All of life is but a day upon the Earth where the human being has the capacity to alter creation and thereby change the place of their soul in Heaven, having marked creation forever. Those who flippantly reduce life down to money and power are destined to be poor in the next world; naked without a garment to stand before the King of Creation—embarrassed before the Creator of Heaven and Earth. What is worthy before the Creator is love and good deeds, compassion, charity, justice, honesty, humility, modesty, the list is endless and each person can take their choice which work to love.

Heaven is rest after work but if you don't work, there is no rest, ever. This world was made for work; children are eager to work until they discover work is hard and children are soft—maturity means work not money. God created a work in the world for everyone to find and to love. Finding the right work is a holy process and love is the devotion, a long road that is short because the process is like foreplay before sex. Every part of life is beautiful and important; every decade of life starting from twenty, is a limb stemming from the Tree of Life—each person is here to bear their fruit.

Seventy years is considered a lifetime, a short amount of time to engrave one's legacy into the firmaments of Heaven through actions upon the Earth. Each life drills into the hard rock of physical existence; some discover a precious stone or living waters on the way to the sea—but each life makes a mark and each life is important. Through this seminal understanding concerning the rules of life, living a good life will cure the world, our Mother Earth, preparing humanity for the coming Thousand Years of Woman and Peace.

Religious authority and scientific skepticism will melt and vanish beneath the Light Zohar emanating from within the BlackWhole. Without senseless dogma or devotion to theory, the eyes of the world will awake and out of the dark pupil of existence, the lowest place in creation, will come a spectacular vision, a vision of the future. In the time of the Temple before being destroyed by Rome, during the seven day celebration in the fall called סוכות/**Succot** the people would become so happy from drinking wine along with sumptuous meals that the entirety would have prophetic visions extending until the end of the six thousand year calendar.

Belief will end, since believing is the answer to the question which can not be answered, so in the absence of a salient explanation, an unsubstantiated belief is offered up to the unsuspecting. Religion and science prey on the true seekers offering themselves up as fodder to the authority who will enslave the mind and harden the heart. Besides institutions, there are bad people in the world interspersed among all nations, some are god-haters others are angry at the Creator because creation does not meet their puny expectations. Lastly, are those who want to stop God's Plan.

The end of the six thousand year calendar is referred to in the Talmud as חבלי משיחי/**Chavli Mechikai-Birth Pangs**. The travail of our times is giving away to beautiful birth, illuminated by Light of Zohar. Everyone in the world will be affected; trees will sing along with the birds, the ground will speak saying, Don't tread on me unless you are walking with God—those dead and buried will grow new bodies impervious to disease or pain, living for a thousand years. Lastly, the Third Temple will descend from the heavens, built from the indestructible to be the beating heart of the world.

The Earth pulses every 26 seconds; the Earth appears to orbit the North Star every 26 thousand years and the Earth is 26 thousand light years from the center of our galaxy where a BlackWhole is responsible for the birth of the stars channelling an interior light caused by a perturbation engraved from a Desire depicted in the Name of God as YHVH with the gematria of 26. The human body when reduced to bone, at peace and covered in dirt takes on the vertical form of the YHVH seeding Mother Earth with the eventual higher human being uniquely etched with lifetimes of experience.

Until the facts of science and the myth of religion met Zohar, the circuit between Heaven and Earth remained broken but once the expanse of the universe is clearly corroborated by scientific inquiry, the Light of Zohar introduces clarity, bringing the world into illumination through this arcane knowledge. The unveiling of Zohar is raining down light upon our world. The Tree of Life is taking hold inside the ground and sprouting, growing and ripening, beginning the new millennium in 220 years, the Thousand Years of Woman and Peace.

ADOM, KINE AND THE SEVEN LANDS

For those yet unconvinced, I present this segment from the זהר חדש/**Zohar Chodesh** also composed two thousand years ago by Rebbe Shimmon ben Yichoi. This segment from the זהר חדש/**Zohar Chodesh** has never been translated into English.

Life in Heaven consists of entities, angels and human souls. Animals derived from angels; entities stem from the first man's relationship with Lilith—human souls are the highest level of life but when invested in a human body, the human being becomes the lowest level, so God can be known in low. The Tree of Life is portrayed in the configuration of the cosmos, the patterning of the Earth and the three triangles comprising the human form. As above, so below. From the original crude human structure was taken the form of man/woman clothed in fire to be tested in the cauldron of free choice and being found lacking were forced to leave.

The ethereal journey from the Garden of Eden took two paths. After 130 years, Adom came directly to Earth where ten generations later, Noah was born a thousand years later. The descendants of Kine had another path, taking them through Seven Lands but seemingly never settled on the Earth, rather made war from Heaven. As recorded in the Book זהר חדש/**Zohar Chodesh**.

מאמר אדם וקין ושבע ארצות
Adom, Kine and the Seven Lands

(1)סדור דעלמה, בשבע קטרין סגלגללן. שבע ארצות אינון, דא לעילא מן דא. כמה דאינון שבע רקיעין, דא לעילא מן דא. ואינון ארץ. אדמה. ארקא. גיא. נשיה. ציה. תבל. לעילא מכלהו, תבל, דכתיב והוא ישפוט תבל בצדק.

The structure of world in seven surrounding orbits. These seven lands are one above another. Similarly, the seven heavens are one above another and these are them: Eretz-Pluto, Adama-Neptune, Arka-

Uranus, Gia-Saturn, Nosia-Jupiter, Tziah-Mars and Tavel-Earth. Highest. from all of them is Tavel, as is written, God judges Tavel with righteousness.

(2) כד נפק אדם מגנתא דעדן, ואתתרך מתמן, אתרמי להההוה דאיקרי ארץ. דאיהו אתר חשיך, דלית תמן נהירו כלום, ולא משמש כלום, כיון דאדם עאל תמן, דחיל דחילו סגי, ולהט החרב המתהפכת, הוה מלהטא גו סטרין, גו ההוא ארץ.

When Adom left the Garden of Eden, pushed out from there by the angels who feared the man might eat from the Tree of Life and therefore live forever; **I will lift him to a place called Eretz-Pluto – a place of darkness. There is no light there at all because the sun does not reach there. When Adom arrived in Eretz/Pluto, he was terrified from the flickering sword** that guarded the Garden of Eden **flashing** erratically **everywhere, upon Eretz-Pluto**. Astronomers know this flickering sword as the Kuiper Belt where Pluto is embedded in darkness accompanied by flashes of light from the erratic movement of chaos.

(3) כיון דנפק שבת, והרהר בתשובה, אריס ליה הקודש ברכהו וסליק ליה לההוא אתר דאקרי אדמה, דכתב וישלחהו י-ה-ו-ה אלהים מגן עדן לעבוד את האדמה. בהאי אית נהירו דנהיר, ודיוקנין דכוכביא ומזלי.

Man was created the afternoon of the Sixth Day of Creation; when the seventh day, the Day of Rest arrived at sunset of the sixth day, light permeated the 24 hours, but **when the שבת/Shabbat ended**, man had to meet the darkness—**repentance went up** in the heart of man, so the **Creator lifted him to a place called Adama-Neptune. As the Torah writes, י-ה-ו-ה אלהים has sent you from the Garden of Eden to work Adoma-Neptune. There, illumination appears as planets and stars**. In Adoma-Neptune, the light from the sun is so far away it looks like a star.

(4) ותמן ציורין דבני נשא עילאין, גוברין דנפקו מאדם קדמאה, במאה ותלתין שנין, דקא הוה משמש ברוחי נוקבי. ואינון עציבין תדיר, ולית בהו חדוה, ואלין מטטי ונפק לעלמה דא, ומהפכין לסטרא בישא, ומהדרן תמן, וצלאן צלותא, ומתיישבן בדוכתייהו תמן. וזרעין זרעין ודרכין ואכלין. וחטין לית תמן, ולא חד משבע זיני תבואה. בהאי אתר, אתיילדו קין והבל.

And there, on Adoma-Neptune, the substance of the **supernal human being** began to take on **form; Strong Ones produced from the First Man during the 130 years** on Adoma-Neptune with Lillith, **There he served the spirit of feminine.** The product of their intercourse gave birth to **depressed** entities **who** were **never happy. They flit about until they come to this world where they turn bad and return from where they came. They say their prayers and dwell in their place** there in Adoma-Neptune. **And here plant producing seeds and they eat, but not wheat nor one from the seven species of fruit. In this place** Adoma-Neptune, **Kine and Hevel were born.**

(5) כיון דחטא קין, אחית ליה הקודש בראך הוא, לההוא אתר דאיקרי ארץ, דכתיב הן גרשת אתי היום מעל פני האדמה, מההוא אתר דאקרי עדמה. והייתי נע ונד בארץ, בגן דתמן אתדחייא ואתתרך, והיה כל מוצאי יהרגני, ההוא להט החרב המתהפכת.

After Kine killed his brother **Hevel, God transported him back to the place called: Eretz-Pluto, as the Torah writes, They** (the angels) **pushed me away this day from the face of the Adoma/Ground. That place is called: Adoma-Neptune. There I will wander about in Eretz-Pluto to where Adom was ejected and distanced from the Garden** of Eden. **And all who find me will kill me** while **the shimmering swords are turning,** preventing return to the Garden of Eden.

(6) והוה דחיל והרהר בתשובה, וסליק ליה הקודש ברוך הוא לארקא, והוה תמן, ואוליד בנין. ובארקא אית נהירו דנהיר מגו שמשא. וזרעין זרעין, ונטעין אילנין, ולית תמן חטין, ולא מאינון שבע זיני תבואה.

Because he was afraid, Kine thought to repent his actions having killed his brother, Havel, **God transported him to** a third world called **Arka-Uranus. There, in Arka-Uranus, Kine birthed children. In Arka-Uranus is** the first world **where the rays of the Sun envelope** this world. **There are seed seeding seeds producing plants and seeds producing trees, but neither wheat nor the Seven Fruits** from the Land of Israel are produced.

(7) כל אינן דתמן, אינון מתולדות קין, ואינון בתרין רישין, מנהון גברין עילאין, ומנהון זעירין. לית להו דעתא שלים כשאר בנשא דהכא. זכאין אינון לזמנין. ולזמנין אהדרן לסטרא בישה, ומולידין ומייתין כשאר בני נשא.

All beings from Arka/Uranus are born from Kine; his offspring have two heads, one large and one small causing a progeny of highly powerful and weakly motivated. **They lack complete knowing like the rest of humankind** souls there on Arka. **And they live and die like the rest of humankind.**

(8) אדם הוה באדמה עד דאוליד שת, ומתמן סליק לעילא, ארבע דרגין מקין. וסליק להאי אתר דאקי תבל, כיון דסליק סליק לאתר בי מקדשא. ותבל דא עילאה על כלהו דרגין דאקרי באינון שמהן דהוה דיוריה בהו. ארץ אדמה הכי, אקרי.

Adom was on Adoma-Neptune until he fathered Shesh; From there he went up four levels from Kine who was on Arka. **He elevated to the place named** תבל/**Tavel-Earth; Since Adom elevated, he went to the place of the Temple** where he had been made then extracted from his original physical body. **תבל/Tavel-Earth is the highest of all** seven **levels and the names where man dwelt is called by: Eretz/Land, and Adoma/Soil.**

(9) דליג אדם תלת דוכתי, גיא, נשיה ציה. גיא איהו אתר, בדוכתא סגי כהאי פותיא ואורכא דגיהנם. בגיא ונשיה וציה אתבדרו אינון דבנו מגדלא, ואולידו תמן. על דארגיזו למלכא עילאה קדישא, נגין דא קריב לנורא דדליק. תמן אית בני נשא בכל יקירו, בעותרא ועפרות זהב, ואבנין יקירין, מאן דעאל תמן והוא מהכא מתבל, בחמידו דההוא עותרא יהבין ליה, ונחית לזמנין לדוכתא דאקרי נשיה, בגין דיתנשי מתמן, וחית להי גיא, דלא ידע אתר דהוא מתמן.

Adom skipped three places: גיא/Gia-Saturn; נשיה/Nosia-Jupiter; ציה/Ztia-Mars. גיא/Gia-Saturn **is a huge place, as wide and deep as** the repository, where the souls transverse life and death, called **Ghinom/Valley Between.** In גיא-Gia/Saturn; נשיה/Nosia/Jupiter; ציה/Ztia-Mars **Those who built the Tower** of Babel **spread out to** גיא/Gia-Saturn; נשיה/Nosia-Jupiter; ציה/Ztia-Mars – there giving birth to children. Since the people of the Tower of Babel angered the High King who is Separate from creation; opposite their war was the fiery flame** burning up the top third of the Tower of Babel. There are people each one wealthy, with riches and gold dust, precious stones; who goes up there from here from Tavel; The preciousness of the wealth will be given to him; but at times he will descend to a place called: Nosia; in order to forget; descending to Gia, knows not from where he came.

(10) גיא, דא הוא באמצעות דעילא ותתא, דא אקרי גי בן הנם, ורצועה חדא נפקא מתמן לעילא להאי תבל, ואקרי אוף הכי גי בן הנם. ותמן פתחא דגיהנם. ואינון בני אנשא דתמן, בגין דא כלהו ידעי בחרשין וחכמאן. ותמן זרעי ונטעי אילנין. ולית תמן חטין, ולא חד משבעה מינין.

גיא/Gia-Saturn is the center between high and low and is therefore called Gi Bain Hinom/Valley Between Them. (The world between the three upper worlds, Tavel-Earth, Tziah-Mars and Nosia-Jupiter; and the three lower worlds, Eretz-Pluto, Adoma-Neptune and Arka-Uranus is Gia-Saturn). **One strand goes out towards Tavel and is called Gi Bain Hinom/Valley Between Them; The opening to Ghinom** (where the souls go prior to Heaven) **is there. The people of Gia/Saturn all know witchcraft and wisdoms. There are seeds and trees there, but no wheat and none of the seven fruits from the Land of Israel.**

(11) בנשיה אית בני נשא קטועין זעירין, ולית להון חוטמין, בר תרין נוקבין, דנפקא בהו רוחא. וכל מה דעבדי, מיד משתכחי. ועל דא איקרי נשיה. וזרעי וטעי אילנין, ולית תמן חטים, ולא משבע זיני.

On Nosia/Jupiter there are swat little people lacking noses, just two holes in their face **to breathe. Whatever they do, they immediately forget; that is why their world is called Nosia/Forget** in Aramaic. **Trees are produced along with wheat, but not the seven kinds** (of fruit from Israel.)

(12) ציה, הוא אתר כשמיה, ביבשותא בכלא. תמן בני נשא שפירן בחיזו. ומגו דההוא ציה, כד ידעי אתר דמקורא דמיין נבעין, עאלין תמן. ולזמנין דסלקין מגו מיין, להאי תבל. ואינון בני מהימנותא יתיר מבני נשא אחרנין, וביניהו דיורין טבן, ועותרא סגי. וזרע זעיר, מגו יבשותא דהתם, ונטעי אילנין ולא מצליחין. ותיאובתא דלהון לבני נשא דהכא.

ציה/Tzia-Dry like the name, this world is completely barren. The people there are beautiful to the eye. Within Tzia-Dry, they know where running water is sourced, they arise there. Sometimes they go up through the water to Tavel. They are skilled beyond other men; life is good and they have much wealth.

Their seed is few because of the dryness there and trees are not successful. There is great envy for these people when they are in Tavel/Earth.

(13) ומכלהו לית דאכלי נהמא, בר אלין דהכא בתבל. דהא לעילא מכל אלין תבל, דכתיב והוא ישפוט תבל בצדק. כגוונא דכל אלין ארעאן, אית בהאי תבל. וכל אלין שמהן אית בהון אוף הכי, בגין דאיהו שביעאה. אית הכא אוף הכי כגוונא דההוא דוכתא דלתתא, וכל אלין בדיורין דבני נשא משניין אלין מאלין, דכתיב מה רבו מעשיך ה'.

In all these seven worlds there is no one who eats bread (means they can not speak) **except in the World of Tavel-Earth. The highest of all these Seven Worlds is Tavel-Earth, as the Torah writes: In Tavel-Earth there is justice** (freedom of choice). **The form of these seven worlds is replicated on Tavel-Earth. Each of the seven land masses is called by the name of the appropriate world. As above, so below. In each of these seven worlds the human being exists; each world is unique and diverse as the Torah writes, What multitude of work, God!**

אבן מאסו
לג בעומר
ה'תשפא

Glossary to Hebrew Terms

כ	י	ט	ח	ז	ו	ה	ד	ג	ב	א
chaf/fak	yod	tet	chet	zayin	vav	hey	dalet	gimmel	vet/bet	alef
ch/k	y	t	ch	z	v	h	d	g	v/b	(silent)

ת	ש	ר	ק	צ	פ	ע	ס	נ	מ	ל
tav	shin	resh	koof	tzade	fey/pey	ayin	samech	nun	mem	lamed
t	s/sh	r	k	tz	f/p	(silent)	s	n	m	l

Hebrew is read from right to left

אגדה/Agada-**Tales**

אדם/Adom-**One Blood**

אממארים/Amoraim-**Expounders**

אהיה/Eheya-**To Be**

אויר/Avir-**Air**

אור/Ore-**Light**

אור אין שוף/OreAinSof-**LightWithoutEnd**

אחד/Echud-**One**

איכה/Iaicha-**Where Are You**

איש/Aish-**Fire**

אלהים/Elohim-**God**

אמת/Emet-**Truth**

ארי/Ari-**Lion**

ארץ/Eretz-**Earth**

אתה/Ata-**You**

בואי כלה/Boi Chala-**Come Bride**

בוצינא דקרדינותא/Botzina Kardinota-**Harder than Hard**

בחכמה/B'Chochma-**With Wisdom**

בני/Beni-**My Child**

בראשית/B'Raishet-**In The Beginning**

בורי/Borai-**Creator**

בחירה חופשית/B'Chira Chofshet-**Free Choice**

ברודים/Brudim-**Separation**

בת קול/Bat Kol-**Daughter of Voice**

גבורה/Gevorah-**Severity**

גליף/Galef-**Engraved**

גמורה/Gemora-**Finishing**

גן עדן/Gan Aden-**Garden of Eden**

די/Di-**Enough**

דין/Din-**Law**

דקה/Daka-**Crushed**

הוד/Hod-**Retreat**

הוה/Hova-**Present**

הטבע/HaTeva-**The Nature**

הטבע/Hatbaya-**Sunken**

היה/Hoya-**Past**

העולם/HaOlam-**The World**

זהר/Zohar-**Brilliance**

זיון/Zion-**Hard**

זכר/Zaakor-**Male**

חבלי משיחי/Chavli Mechikai-**Birth Pangs**

חברים/Chaverim-**Friends**

חומש/Chomesh-**Five**

חזיר/Chazir-**Return**

חרות/Choret-**Etched**

חרות/Choret-**Free**

טרוף/Trope-**Infliction**

יהודי/Yehudi-**Jew**

יהיה/Yehiya-**Future**

יום קיפור/Yom Kipur-**Day of Atonement**

ים/Yaam-**Sea**

יסוד/Yesod-**Foundation**

ירידות הדורת/Yridut HaDorat-**Descension of Generations**

ישראל/Yisroel-**Israel**

כבוד/Covid-**Respect**

כח/Choach-**Power**

כלה/Calah-**Betrothed**

כתבים/Kotivim-**Writings**

כתר/Keter-**Crown**

לב/Lev-**Heart**

ליכה/Lecha-**Walking**

מאד/Moad-**More**

מגדל/Migdol-**Tower of Babel**

מדות/Medot-**Measurements**

מדרש/Midrash-**Exposition**

מהלך/MaHaluch-**Walker**

מוקם פני/Mokem Ponoi-**Empty Space**

מים/Mayim-**Water**

מלך המות/Melech Hamovit-**Angel of Death**

מלכות/Malchut-**Royalt**

מצבתה/Matzavta-**Gravestone**

משנה/Mishna-**Teacher**

נבויים/Neviem-**Prophets**

נצח/Netzak-**Victory**

נקדה/Nekoda-**Sound**

נקודה/Nikuda-**BlackWhole**

נשי/Noshim-**Female**

סגי אור/Sogi Ore-**Too Much Light**

סוף ימים/Sof Yamim-**End of Days**

ספר יצירה/Sefer Yitzira-**Book of Form**

עיטרא/Atira-**Crown**

עברי/Evri-**Beyond the River**

עיקב משיחי/Achaiv Mechichai-**Heels of Redemption**

עיץ חים/Etz Chiam-**Tree of Life**

עקודים/Akudim-**Lines**

עשר ספירות/Eser Sephirot-**Ten Luminaries**

פלה/Pelah-**Wonderous**

ציא/Ztia-**Dry**

צמצון הראשון/Ztmzton HaRishon-**First Contraction**

קבלה/Cabala-**Recieve**

קיננריט/Kinneret-**Harp**

קתר/Keter-**Crown**

ראח/Ruach-**Spirit**

ראש/Rosh-**Head**

ראש השנה/Rosh HaShana-**New Year**

רעיא מהימנא/Riyah Mehemna-**Faithful Shepherd**

רצה ושוב/Rutzi V'Shaav-**Running and Returning**

רקיעים/Rikiem-**Heavens**

שבת/Shabbat-**Rest**

שלום/Shalom-**Peace**

שופר/Shofar-**Ram's Horn**

שבת/Shabbat-**Rest**

שטן/Satan-**Opposer**

שמים/Shamiam-**Heaven**

שם הגודל/Shem HaGodal-**The Great Name**

שער השמים/Shar HaShamiam-**The Gates of Heaven**

תהו/Tohu-**Chaos**

תהלים/Tihilim-**Psalms**

תורה/Torah-**Teaching**

תורה של כתב/Shel Kitav-**Written Torah**

תורה של פאה/Shel Peh-**Oral Torah**

תבל/Tavel-**Earth**

תיקון/Tikun-**Fixing**

תלמוד/Talmud-**Learn**

תניים/Tenoiyim-**Techers**

www.ingramcontent.com/pod-product-compliance
Lightning Source LLC
Chambersburg PA
CBHW070859080526
44589CB00013B/1137